SUPERNATURAL
IN THE WEST

GW00703272

Michael Williams

BOSSINEY BOOKS

First published in 1996 by Bossiney Books, St Teath, Bodmin, Cornwall.

Typeset and printed by Penwell Ltd, Callington, Cornwall.

© Michael Williams

ISBN 1 899383 03 4

ACKNOWLEDGEMENTS

Front cover photography: Roy Westlake

Back cover photography: Julia Davey

Other photography: Ray Bishop

Drawings: Felicity Young

Front cover design: Maggie Ginger

About the Author – and the book

MICHAEL WILLIAMS is the best known ghost hunter in the South West. He has been investigating hauntings and different aspects of the paranormal for more than thirty years. He is the Ghost Club Society's investigator in the region, and has broadcast, lectured and written extensively on supernatural subjects since 1975. His recent publications include **Psychic Phenomena** *and* **Edge of the Unknown,** *and in 1995 he appeared in a series entitled* **The Mysterious West** *on Westcountry Television.*

A Cornishman, Michael Williams has been publishing for more than twenty years. He and his wife Sonia live in a cottage on the shoulder of a green valley outside St Teath in North Cornwall. Outside his Bossiney activities, he is a writing and publishing consultant, evaluating manuscripts and advising writers on their publishing prospects.

In addition to publishing and writing, Michael is a keen cricketer and collector of cricket books and autographs. He was the first captain of the Cornish Crusaders Cricket Club and is today President of the Crusaders. He is also a member of Cornwall and Gloucestershire County Cricket Clubs – and a Vice-President of the Cornwall Rugby Football Union. A member of the International League for the Protection of Horses and the RSPCA, he has worked hard for reform in laws relating to animal welfare.

In **Supernatural in the West** *he explores a wide range of paranormal activity – ghosts and ghost hunting, healing with crystals and candle burning, déjà vu and disappearances and animal experiences are some of the subjects – and many of the illustrations are appearing in book form for the first time.*

SUPERNATURAL IN THE WEST

A Westcountryman, a sober reliable workman, married in his mid twenties, yet within a few weeks of his marriage he came home drunk. His wife was bewildered because it was so out of character. A few weeks later it happened again, and after the third drunken bout his young wife invited a 'white witch' to visit their cottage. The wise woman did something very surprising. She advised the young woman to burn an armchair which had been given as a wedding present. When the chair was burned, the husband's drinking escapades stopped as abruptly as they had begun. Apparently the armchair had originally been the property of a drunkard who had committed suicide sitting in it.

Here in the West we have a number of religious ghosts. The George & Pilgrim Hotel, Glastonbury, has a ghost monk, a fat and cheerful character, who has been seen by a number of visitors. Monks in grey have walked St Nectan's Glen near Tintagel since the reign of Queen Victoria and in North Devon there have been reports of St Nectan himself haunting the churchyard at Stoke near Hartland. In all three locations the ghosts disappear as suddenly as they appear.

A quite different case was that of a young man from Bristol who worked as an assistant in the Central Library, College Green, Bristol. It was around mid-September 1938, the time of the Munich crisis, and the young man went on holiday to Exmoor. He never came back – and was last seen on the foreshore at Lynmouth.

From an eerie disappearance to a mysterious appearance – or reappearance – in December 1995. Two men, out rabbit hunting near Bishopsteignton in Devon, saw a black panther-like animal.

Had the Beast of Bodmin Moor strayed? Later I shall be devoting a chapter to the continuing saga of strange animals roaming the countryside in the west.

On to strange sightings in the sky. In November 1995 a pink triangular object tipped with red lights hovered over Pool in Cornwall. Seen by as many as eight people, it was clearly no hallucination of some highly imaginative individual, and a fortnight later six witnesses at Trispen near Truro observed 'an elongated object with brightly lit portholes.' The triangular pink light seen in the Redruth area circled a disused engine house and chimney stack and, according to eye-witnesses, floated not more than thirty-five feet off the ground without making a sound.

Ghostly manifestation is another ongoing matter in the Westcountry. From time to time I come across hauntings – relating to manifestations which have appeared and reappeared in one form or another over a period of many years.

Only this morning I talked with Irene Butt of the New Inn, Coleford near Crediton in Devon. This fourteenth-century inn has

THE NEW INN at Coleford near Crediton is a haunted inn with a difference. Its ghost defies neat classification. Some say the phantom is a monk; others say he is a man who died in the 1914-18 war . . . and there have been other unusual happenings here. The New Inn is a thirteenth century listed building of considerable character and the resident parrot 'Captain' greets you on your arrival.

PAR BEACH on the south coast of Cornwall on a September morning. This lovely stretch of sand on the rim of St Austell Bay is in the heart of Daphne du Maurier's Cornwall. Her stories often had an eerie twist, and it is an established fact that many ghosts manifest themselves near water. Our old seamen were a very superstitious race, and in the days of sail omens had a special significance: days and nights when men and their vessels were at the mercy of gales and storms. The coastline of Cornwall is littered with shipwrecks.

a ghost which defies classification. Some say he is a monk called Sebastian; others say he is 'Mabel's brother who died in the 1914-1918 war.' Irene Butt told me: 'Personally I have not seen any ghost in our eight years here, but various strange things have happened at the New Inn . . . quite small things but they invariably happen when we are full. Guns over the fireplace have fallen from the wall and moved a surprisingly long distance. We've had bottles jumping off shelves . . . sometimes bottles exploding and falling on the floor.

'We have a corridor and one particular bedroom. I find it a perfectly normal friendly corridor but we had a teenage girl who worked here . . . she had a bedroom off it . . . and she didn't like it.

'In 1994 we had a gentleman staying here, and he slept in this particular bedroom . . . yes, it is quite a cold bedroom, in fact it's the coldest room in the building . . . and he was woken during the night: a light at the foot of his bed and then the light moved around the room. He was also conscious of a strong sense of smell, a very pleasant perfume, and was aware of the presence of a female. After a while he sat up in bed and then the light and the scent disappeared. But he was quite sure it had not been a dream experience.'

The Westcountry is full of strange cases and, despite all the investigation and analysis that has gone on, to a degree it remains the Unknown Country.

I have been exploring the supernatural in the west – and beyond – for more than thirty years and what rewarding years they have been. Robert Louis Stevenson may have been right about it being better to travel hopefully than to arrive, but I have travelled hopefully *and* arrived at some fascinating supernatural destinations – and conclusions.

Supernatural, I suppose, means different things to different people. *Collins English Dictionary* gives it as many as five definitions. I particularly like the first: '. . . of or relating to things that cannot be explained according to natural laws.'

In this case I see the *supernatural* as a broad title, bringing together varying events of psychic phenomena and people relating to those events here in the region.

In some chapters the emphasis is on *mystery*. The Beast of Bodmin Moor, for example, is not a supernatural character – or characters – but he is certainly a four-legged figure of considerable mystery. Likewise the disappearances belong to the realm of the mysterious rather than the paranormal.

In *Supernatural in the West* I have concentrated on Bossiney publishing territory which is approximately a line from Bristol across to Bournemouth and all the way down to Cornwall. The great majority of these cases are appearing inside a Bossiney title for the first time, and where I have returned to an earlier theme I have done so for a fuller treatment or because new information has been unearthed. Now and then I have gone beyond Bossiney's defined publishing boundaries for the sake of providing something more comprehensive by adding new dimensions.

I wonder for example, how many people know about the work of Louis de Wohl during the Hitler war. A German astrologer, with

Jewish blood, he had come to London four years before the outbreak of war, and during it his services were employed by the British for counter-propaganda. The idea behind using this gifted German was simple yet shrewd. The British knew the Nazis were using astrology in planning their military strategy; therefore knowledge of the kind of advice they were being given meant an important step ahead of the enemy.

The notion that the human mind can transcend our five senses is ancient, but the scientific exploration of the theory is relatively modern. Dreams which turn into reality, the premonition which transforms into a living disaster, the eerie knowledge that we have been here *before*: psychic phenomena have fascinated for a long time – and we are now in the midst of a revolution.

Today men and women of ability and integrity are working on the supernatural – and a great deal is happening here in the west. Only a fool would refuse to acknowledge the fact there are forces about which we know relatively little and over which we have no control whatsoever.

This century, especially the last fifty years, has seen an incredible accumulation of paranormal evidence, and most serious students of the subject believe that in the twenty-first century we shall learn to harness the supernatural and employ the untapped potential which lies within us.

That is an exciting prospect.

December 1995

REFLECTIONS
OF A GHOST HUNTER

I CAN precisely pinpoint the beginning of my ghost hunting: Midsummer Eve 1965. The last thirty years have seen important changes in ghost hunting. No longer do we expect to see phantoms in only traditional haunts like churches and castles, along lonely country roads or on the seashore – of course, manifestations do continue to occur in such places. But there have been sightings by reliable witnesses in quite mundane circumstances at modern locations.

Ghosts have been seen in council houses, on buses, in public lavatories and on aircraft. Moreover these psychic encounters have been experienced by a wide range of personalities. My files on the subject contain letters from academics and farmworkers, housewives and musicians, old and young, rich and poor. Recent correspondence has come from a lady solicitor, a television interviewer, a former member of the old Rhodesian police force, a housewife with a special interest in UFOs, a spiritual healer with a particular gift for healing animals, and a retired motor mechanic.

The ghosts of Britain and particularly those in the Westcountry are remarkably varied. I never travel along the A38 in the vicinity of Wellington, Somerset, without thinking of the phantom hitchhiker who, torch in hand, attempts to flag down motorists at night. There have been detailed descriptions of this male ghost – one motorist who gave him a lift one very wet night actually engaged in conversation with his strange passenger. Moreover about four weeks later the same motorist picked up the same hitchhiker in equally dreadful conditions. Why anyone should seek a lift in such terrible weather not once, but twice is incredible. Perhaps even more incredibly the conversation between the motorist and his drenched passenger followed their earlier pattern.

It was the celebrated ghost hunter Tom Corbett who said: 'Ghosts cannot be put on the witness stand, or have their fingerprints taken.'

That may be so, but more and more of us are veering to the view that the twenty-first century may well produce evidence proving the reality – and the nature – of ghosts. There may be more than one explanation because of the variety of ghostly manifestation. Roughly, there are four types of ghost: A: Ghosts of living people, admittedly a minority. B: Crisis ghosts who manifest themselves to relations and close friends when they are going through a crisis or are on the verge of leaving this world. C: Post-mortem ghosts who appear after death and are not to be confused with category B. D: Ghosts who are observed by people who have no connection with them and can be seen years after death. And, of course, there are classifications within these categories – and beyond them. There are animal ghosts, there are haunted objects – and anniversary manifestations or spirits who return at regular or fairly regular intervals. Interestingly too there are ghosts who cease to haunt. In their case they may have no wish to return to this world and are quite happy to settle 'on the other side' as the Spiritualists would say.

The poet Robert Graves may have got somewhere near the truth when he ventured this belief: ghosts are events rather than things or creatures. I certainly think time slip experiences come within Mr Graves's definition. The term 'time slip' means when we find ourselves 'in the past'. On such occasions a whole paranormal scene may unfold. My records contain accounts of religious ceremonies at Glastonbury, a duel to the death down on the Lizard peninsula in South Cornwall, a squadron of Roman soldiers marching over Bindon Hill to the east of Lulworth Cove on the Dorset coast, a funeral procession of monks in white robes moving through Wistman's Wood on Dartmoor – these are only some examples of time slips.

According to a survey carried out in 1980 44 per cent of British people interviewed believe in the existence of ghosts. As many as one in seven said they had seen or heard something of a supernatural nature. The same poll also showed over half the population believed in some form of psychic phenomena. A poll, carried out in

GHOSTLY procession of monks: Wistman's Wood, Dartmoor

the United States around the same time, revealed that over half the American population – 57 per cent of adult men and women – believed in the existence of ghosts. I happen to believe similar surveys today would see no decline in those figures – in fact they may well be even higher.

Let us assume – and it's a pretty harsh assumption – that nine people out of ten are mistaken or are lying (though why they should baffles me), the remaining one per cent represents a solid body of evidence.

We must not forget presences either. On a number of occasions one feels the presence of an invisible companion – and I am not thinking of the working of a vivid imagination. In his autobiography, published in 1919, the famous polar explorer Sir Ernest Shackleton wrote how during the 'long and racking' 36-hour march he made with two colleagues over the glaciers of South Georgia, 'it seemed to me often that we were four, not three.' Sir Ernest said nothing of this presence at the time, but later the two other men admitted they had had the same awareness – so much so that he admitted 'the dearth of human words, the roughness of mortal speech' in trying to describe what they had felt; 'but a record of our journeys would be incomplete without reference to a subject very near to our hearts.'

Having heard supernatural sounds at three different locations in North Cornwall, I am inclined to think many of us at some time or another hear sounds of a paranormal nature without being aware of their nature. I once interviewed a man who had heard a plane coming to land on an airfield when, in reality, that particular aircraft had crashed earlier in the day. It is only when this kind of revelation strikes that we understand the significance. Recently a reader from Thomas Hardy Country in Dorset kindly sent me details of a piano which played of its own accord at the Crown Hotel, Poole. On one occasion at The Crown six people heard the old piano, then stored in a loft, '. . . single notes were struck one at a time . . . the impression was as if a child was striking the keyboard with just one finger.' They went to the loft but nobody was there, yet the piano continued to play more notes. Had they not gone to the loft they would have assumed a child was enjoying himself or herself experimenting at the old piano.

GHOSTLY music at the Crown Hotel, Poole.

FELICITY YOUNG on the heights of Dartmoor. Over the years Felicity has produced more than a hundred paranormal illustrations for Bossiney making her one of the most prolific illustrators in this field of British publishing. Her ghostly drawings have ranged from a stone age warrior riding a shaggy horse in Dorset to a human being dressed in a one-piece silver suit and a spaceman's helmet at Pont near Fowey, Cornwall, and a great deal more including a black retriever dog who has been seen from time to time in Wiltshire and girlish wraiths prancing and leaping on the foreshore in Lulworth Cove at night.

'Ghostly drawings are very different from conventional drawings,' she says, 'in that they require a great deal more imagination. Though, of course, I pick up a good deal of detail from reading the relevant parts of the manuscript. Some of the eye-witness accounts are so detailed that they leap out at you. In many cases you understand these people have had real experiences with very clear sighting like the Wiltshire case where the animal is not described as a black dog, any black dog, but a black **retriever**. *Then you get groups of people like the Roman warriors in one account and there is the strange case of the haunted Morris car at Melksham in Wiltshire with its strange roof passengers, four girls one of whom has long black hair, long black gloves and very little else!*

'I particularly enjoyed doing a feminine hand sparkling with rings, hovering between an old-fashioned lamp and a will. I like doing animals, especially the white donkey of Studley in Dorset . . . the variety of ghosts is quite incredible.'

VARIOUS PRESENCES have been felt inside the Bedford Hotel, Tavistock, and they must be friendly spirits because there is a warm and friendly atmosphere here. In this, the reception area of the hotel, members of staff have had strange experiences, notably in the early hours of the morning. It is an undeniable fact hotels and inns have a high percentage of manifestations. The Bedford, in fact, occupies a very historic Tavistock site. Here once stood Tavistock Abbey, built in the tenth century. When Henry VIII dissolved the monasteries in the mid 1400s, the Duke of Bedford became the recipient of the monastery buildings – and he promptly demolished most of them. Charles I stayed here. Consequently there is a strong sense of the past in and around the hotel.

Do ghost hunters require special qualities?

Peter Underwood, the Life President of the Ghost Club Society, in his excellent book *The Ghost Hunter's Guide*, published by Blandford Press of Poole, Dorset in 1986, wrote: 'What makes a sincere and responsible ghost hunter? . . . he or she should be a mixture of the best kind of detective and the best kind of investigative reporter with something of the scientist and something of the psychologist thrown in . . .'

That very fine novelist Muriel Spark once referred to 'the invisible third ear,' an ability to pick up things below the material surface of twentieth century things. Perhaps some psychic characters have a 'third eye' whereby they are able to see *other* things. They trust their sixth sense as well as their other five.

It is an odd fact that sometimes people, who have a ghostly sighting, are not on any psychical wavelength at that precise moment. When I was driving along the Camelford – Bodmin road and saw a phantom cyclist my thoughts were on a new Bossiney book and how it was likely to be a good seller in the shops on the run-up to Christmas. When I interviewed a man called Alan Sandry about an eerie sighting near Little Petherick I asked him this question: 'Were you thinking you might encounter this strange object?' Alan smiled and said: 'I'll tell you what I was thinking about. I was thinking about some shares and what a rotten price they were!'

On supernatural investigations I have never felt nervous or afraid – tense, a little apprehensive perhaps – and I say that out of no sense of boasting: merely a fact. In my opinion the lack of fear in many paranormal situations is due to this: often only *later* does the observer fully understand the significance of the happening. A figure may disappear through a solid wall or simply vanish into thin air; a dog may appear in the middle of a road – be there one moment and gone the next. A light may gradually wane and then, darkness. *Until that moment of revelation* the observer has assumed everything normal and rooted in the here and now.

Not everything though happens quietly and placidly. Back in the 1920s the writer Beverley Nichols, his brother and an Oxford University friend Lord Peter Audries, one evening visited a haunted house called Castel Mare in Middle Warberry Road, Torquay, South Devon. They found the dilapidated, empty property oppressive rather than frightening – murder had been committed there. Beverley Nichols, alone in the upper hall, had a curious sensation. Waiting for his two companions, 'a black film seemed to cover the left side of his brain, as if he were being anaesthetised.' He staggered outside into the open air before fainting. At a later stage Nichols was joined by his brother and Peter Audries continued to explore the building alone. Every few minutes he whistled to indicate all was well. Suddenly the whistles stopped and the Nichols brothers had the feeling that someone or something had rushed past them out of the house. They rushed to the window and heard sounds of a struggle and more cries. When Lord Audries reappeared he was dishevelled and covered in plaster dust. He had been knocked to the ground and had to summon all his strength to crawl downstairs and into the garden. Upstairs he had experienced a profound sense of evil, but on reaching the foot of the stairs the oppression left him. Later the three men learnt a double murder had taken place in the old bathroom: the doctor then in residence killing first his wife and then a maid.

Poltergeist activity perhaps, rather than a ghost.

In investigating a supernatural matter at Altarnun on the edge of Bodmin Moor I met Harry Cleverly, a medium who lives in the village. Before settling in Cornwall, Harry Cleverly was a housing officer for the council in Lambeth, London, and he told me of some tenants who in 1980 were squatting in a certain property. 'They had left their original accommodation claiming it was haunted. So I went along to interview them. They told me of frightening experiences, things being thrown around the house. We went back to the first property and in the bedroom I was immediately aware of a poltergeist presence. I told this entity to go away, but as soon as I turned around to leave the room I came face to face with the presence. Nothing to be seen, but as a medium I knew it was still there and had little intention of leaving.

'Eventually the matter went to court and at a critical point in the proceedings the judge asked me 'Is this place haunted?'

'I had no hesitation in replying: 'Yes. It is haunted.'

'The judge promptly dropped the case, and I later carried out an exorcism at the house during which I went into a trance, and the

HARRY CLEVERLY tells Carole Evans of his strange encounters in the ▶ *Cornish village of Altarnun. He has seen a female ghost walk straight through this churchyard gate which was firmly shut at the time. He has also seen a Victorian parson in a frock coat at Penhallow Manor and a woman, wearing a 1930s apron, cleaning the hearth in his cottage.*

entity left. It was all natural enough. He was a previous owner who cared about the place and didn't like the idea of builders coming in and altering the property, which was the council's intention. Anyway the exorcism worked and peace returned.'

Harry had another interesting experience. 'Quite an amusing case,' he recalls. 'This woman found the contents of her fridge spread all over the kitchen floor each morning. She didn't come back to me after I'd done my exorcism so hopefully it worked.'

On the subject of ghosts in general he says: 'I tell people don't be frightened by them. They cannot and will not do you any harm. I suppose the worst thing a ghost could do is frighten you to the extent of giving you a heart attack. But that's not the ghost's fault.Usually they are very peaceful characters.'

Looking back to the first half of this century, through reading and research I get the impression the old scientists were a pretty conceited lot believing they had all the answers. But as we approach the twenty-first century more and more intelligent people are laying aside the blinkers of conventional thinking and beginning to regard the ancient distinction between natural and supernatural as almost meaningless.

In a way, we have been travelling through a century of curious contradiction. Ours is a chapter – or chapters- of space travel and scientific progress. That is one side of the coin. The other is the vast catalogue of happenings which defy all logical explanation – in the realm we call the supernatural.

Claire Wolferstan is a psychic and a writer with a difference. Her gift has nothing to do with traditional 'automatic writing.' It all began in 1973 and in Claire's own words '. . . I very soon learnt to "hear" the dictation in my inner mind; so it's telepathy between the third and fourth dimension.'

For the purpose of this publication I asked her to obtain the answer to this very specific question: 'Will the reality and nature of ghosts be proved in the next century?'

Here is Claire's reply received from 'out there:'

'The answer to this question put briefly, is yes. To give further enlightenment on this theme it should be understood that Earth's electrical impulses are heightened, as indeed are those of the other members of the solar system. This process although of necessity

CLAIRE WOLFERSTAN photographed with her late husband James. Her findings in the spirit world give great encouragement for ghost hunters in the next century when there could be a major breakthrough.

extremely slow as regarded by people on Earth, will mean that visitants from "the next world", the fourth dimension, call it what you will, will operate on a "wavelength" that is closer to Earth's. As a result the particles of which the heavenly visitor is composed will be the more easily discerned by humans. Here again as now, those humans known as sensitives will be enabled to see them more readily than those who are less psychic. As the century advances so it will become easier and easier for communication between the two dimensions, so that even the most sceptical will be obliged to accept there is life after death, and a great burden will have been lifted from mankind.

'It should be understood that the ghostly apparitions, as experienced under prevailing conditions, fall into very different categories, for some are, as has already been surmised, mere reflections of the past re-enacted by a set of circumstances conducive to their perception by a human, or humans, on the current time scale. These circumstances can be in part climatic for the necessary electrical impulses to operate, and in part due to human intervention, and here too the human contribution is of an electrical nature, for as is known, every living thing has its own electric forcefield and this forcefield can be drawn upon by phantoms of whichever category.

'The commonest category of ghostly visitants is that of the astral replica of a dead person appearing in scenes once familiar to him or her. These visitors from the fourth dimension vary enormously in their intent. The unfortunate few are unaware of their transition to the next world and cling to earthly scenes. These should be helped by prayer to God that they may be taken to their rightful place in heaven.

'There are, however, human entities who for different reasons, to be discussed later, wish to return to familiar, earthly scenes although they are now discarnate. They will return in their "astral" forms ie that replica form of their earthly selves, albeit perfect, with

I CAME to know Bristol in 1952 when doing the major part of my ▶
National Service at the old Horfield Barracks. It was not until 1965
that I began investigating the supernatural but in those earlier days I
formed the impression that Bristol, in places, was an eerie city. Now and
then you felt you were caught up in some kind of time warp.

which God provides His children in which to operate in 'the hereafter', when the physical body has expired. These astral bodies are composed of finer material operating at a higher speed than is known in the physical world of man, and require to draw strength of an electrical nature from the surroundings and in particular from incarnate beings in order to materialise on Earth. This process incidentally, explains the sudden drop in temperature whenever a ghostly manifestation is attempted, or indeed achieved.

'It will be seen therefore that under prevailing conditions on Earth it is unlikely that the discarnate one will be enabled to manifest for any length of time owing to the extreme difficulties experienced in harnessing the electrical forces needed.

'To expatiate further on the reasons why discarnates choose this difficult undertaking, it should be understood they are many and very varied. One of the commonest is that of affection for a certain location where the entity once enjoyed life, such as a certain room or a favourite garden, library or meeting place with friends.

'Another reason is the affection felt for those they have left behind on Earth, and in some cases they wish to convey a message as to some unfinished business, or even to right a wrong. Here they will experience extreme difficulty in communicating unless there happens to be a medium or a "sensitive" present. It may even take years to establish a link, by which time the matter may no longer be relevant on Earth, though it still seems of import to the discarnate for whom time will have assumed an entirely different meaning.

'Other appearances can be due to a certain curiosity as to what is taking place in the one time environment of the discarnate one, often accompanied by the desire to be recognized or acknowledged by incarnate beings. These latter ones are not generally very highly evolved souls, tending to cling to earthly memories rather than enjoy the delights and opportunities offered them in heavenly spheres.

'It will be seen therefore, that in all categories the individual is operating under the Law of Free Will, which operates throughout the universe.'

DEEPER INTO
THE SUPERNATURAL

THINGS are not always what they seem. We are sitting in a railway carriage standing in a station. Looking through the window we see another train, also standing. Suddenly we become aware of our train pulling out of the station, another stage of our journey has begun. The windows of the train opposite are running swiftly across our view but then comes a doubt. We look towards the platform windows and make a discovery: our carriage is stationary. It is the *other* train which is moving.

Hearing too can be peculiar. There was the case of Admiral Lord St Vincent who, when staying with his sister, did not hear strange sounds that were terrifying her. Only when she summoned up the courage to tell her brother did he begin to hear them as well.

Late one summer evening a gentleman residing on the Lizard peninsula was walking home after a drink or two at his local inn when he became convinced that 'a supernatural something was ahead of me to the side of the lane. I could see this odd shape and hear strange noises,' he told me, 'and I was very nervous about passing it. But eventually I screwed up the courage to carry on walking, and when I came to this "supernatural something" it turned out to be a pig sleeping and snoring in the hedge!'

Peter Underwood, author of several Bossiney bestsellers on Westcountry ghosts, has reflected: 'I have long been of the opinion that ninety-eight per cent of reported hauntings have a natural explanation, but it is the other two per cent that has interested me for half a century.' Peter, a Fellow of the Royal Society of Arts, is the ghost hunter par excellence in Britain today.

Sometimes a genuine ghost account has a sequel, on other occasions one wishes the person who had experienced the sighting had investigated a little more fully. One such account, containing both these ingredients, came to me via a correspondent in Avon who called it 'The Woman in Black' story.

'My friend Roy, a marine and car engineer, once worked in France for ten years. His mother joined him one Christmas, and whilst they were entertaining some guests they heard steps coming up the stairs leading to Roy's flat. There came a knock at the door but when he opened it there was no-one to be seen. However a voice asked for the woman in black. "She's not here," said Roy (in French I suppose!) and shut the door to the surprise of all. A few days later his mother was standing at the flat window to watch Roy cross La Place on his way to work when suddenly she felt there was someone in the room. Turning round she saw a woman in black sitting at the table. Asked what she was doing there the woman vanished.

'To his surprise Roy met his mother wandering about the town later on, and she explained she had been thoroughly unnerved by the ghostly appearance of the woman in black. No explanation was found I'm afraid. I don't think they even tried – a pity.'

One of the oddest paranormal facts in the Westcountry concerns Lulworth Castle in Dorset. For many years 'a luminous spot' on the wall of a bedroom there could not be removed – not even reshaping of the masonry shifted it. The castle was burned down in 1929 and is now merely a ruin.

Dorset, for all its orderly beauty, is a county peppered in manifestations. Antony D Hippisley Coxe, when researching his book *Haunted Britain*, came to this conclusion: 'I have chosen Dorchester as a centre because it is the hub of an area which is full of mystery . . . within a radius of twenty miles there are more than two dozen sites.'

There is an amusing ghost story about St Peter's Church in the town reputed to be haunted by Nathaniel Templeman, a former

CHURCHYARDS may vary in their character and atmosphere, but in them you inevitably think about life and death. In their differing ways they challenge belief and disbelief. Not surprising then that many manifestations have been seen in and around churchyards. ▶

rector. One year, two churchmen, after putting up the Christmas decorations, decided to reward and refresh themselves with some Communion wine. The ghost suddenly appeared and 'put the fear of God' into them.

A Bossiney reader in Wiltshire wrote to me about a strange aircraft experience near Stonehenge. He wrote: 'Near Stonehenge is a monument dedicated to two airmen who died in the vicinity in 1912, when their plane crashed. They were Captain Lorraine and Staff Sergeant Wilson, and they have rather special places in service history, in that they were the very first members of the old Royal Flying Corps to perish. Then just before D-Day in World War Two Sir Michael Bruce was driving past Stonehenge when he – and others travelling with him – saw a plane crash into a nearby wood. Naturally they began an immediate search in the hope of finding any survivors but all they found was the memorial: no sign of an aircrash or any airmen.'

It is interesting how ghostly coaches and horsedrawn vehicles have become appreciably rarer since the appearance and multiplication of the motor car. Though phantom horses continue to be seen and, above all, heard, the sound of hoofbeats is a relatively frequent manifestation. We have not though reached a stage where many ghostly aircraft appear – as distinct from UFOs – in any significant number, though it is fair to assume the airborne pattern could change in the future, when more and more people will choose flying instead of driving cars along crowded roads.

I have a special liking for the air of mystery which many woods generate; the belief that certain trees are haunted has a long tradition. That very perceptive writer Elliott O'Donnell devoted an entire book to the theme. In his *Trees of Ghostly Dread*, published in 1958, he had this to say: 'To the mind that is at all imaginative there is often something very ghostly in the appearance of trees in the dusk; their fantastically fashioned, knotted and gnarled branches can bear such an unpleasant resemblance to bony arms with long, curved fingers outstretched, as if in readiness to pounce on

AMONG Bristol's ghosts is a former Duchess of Beaufort on horseback. ▶

one. The rustling of the leaves as a breeze stirs them sounds like whispering voices, and the singing and moaning of the wind like the crying and wailing of lost souls.'

From countryside to a notable Westcountry city: Bristol. I did most of my National Service in the Army at Horfield Barracks back in the early 1950s. Though not then into supernatural investigation, I nevertheless formed the definite impression that in places Bristol was a spooky place. More than forty years on, I am not in the least surprised it boasts many ghosts. The black-robed monk, seen in and around All Saints Church, the limping boy ghost at the Llandogger Trow Inn, the long dead Duchess of Beaufort riding on horseback, a phantom cat called 'Smokey' – these are just four of the many ghosts seen around the city. Bristol's 'other population' is numerous and various, and, of course, it was on a visit to Bristol that Montague Summers saw his sadly misshapen girl ghost. Summers, a Roman Catholic priest, was an expert on subjects like witchcraft and vampires; he encountered this hunchbacked pale-faced girl haunting the house where she had lived her short unhappy life until she committed suicide in the mid 1800s.

Back here in Cornwall another haunting and a curious coincidence. Linda Berry, who is the co-ordinator of the Cornish Psychic Research Group, invited me to speak to her members in September 1995, and told me of her haunting experiences at her bungalow Jonlyn, Canonstown near Hayle in West Cornwall. I had lived there for a while during the last war before moving to the bungalow next door when it became vacant. She told me:

'In the summer of 1988 we moved into a bungalow in Canonstown. It was over the next year that members of the family witnessed a man walking around the back of the house. We live in a bungalow with a drive that goes straight to the back garden, it is therefore not unusual for people to go round to the back of the house to find a way in. We were so convinced each time that the man was real, as he passed the lounge window that someone always got up to greet the visitor, only to find that no one was there.

'My brother and sister, both visitors to the house, had seen him, whilst they were outside in the garden, he was making the same journey, around the house. As far as I know, he never deviated from that path. The last time I saw him, it was the clearest glimpse I ever had of him. I was in the garden. I saw a man moving at a fast walk, he appeared tall, and dressed in black, and disappeared as he passed the corner to the back of the house, I was with my brother and sister at the time. He has not appeared to my knowledge since then, so I believe he must have gone.'

THE LIZARD peninsula has a strong sense of the past. Is this why the Lizard, in places, has such a haunting and haunted air? This old photograph, taken in 1908, is real enough, and it has timeless quality. Daniel Farson is one author on the supernatural who believes a ghost could be **'a footprint on time.'**

CANDLE BURNING

IF someone were to ask me about vivid early childhood memories, candles would be among them. Perhaps not surprising then that in later life I should have started exploring the supernatural, for candle burning is a simple yet significant magical art.

I may be wrong but candle magic probably starts for most of us with the early ritual of blowing out the candles on our birthday cake. Assuming that is the case, then we are unknowingly following two key principles. First, we concentrate by blowing out the candles on top of the cake, and then comes our wishing – our magical desire. Serious students of the occult believe it is our willpower which makes the dream come true.

My first awareness of candles having a magical quality was back in the early 1960s when I interviewed Ithel Colquhoun, the painter and writer, at her home at Paul high above Mount's Bay. Clearly she had lit them for our interview in the expectation they would create a good atmosphere for it. In retrospect I can see the interview did go well.

Years later a 'wise woman' from North Cornwall told me how she believed candles could predict the future. 'If a candle's reluctant to light, then a storm is on its way,' she said. 'If it gutters in a room where there are no draughts, bad weather is coming. If a candle flame burns blue, it foretells a frost or even a death.' On important occasions, like births and marriages, she advised lighting candles 'to ward off evil spirits.'

When we think about the candle historically we see it has been a vital source of light for men and women and a powerful symbol of comfort. The old teachers and preachers believed there was a

spark of divine light inside each individual which could be fanned into 'a spiritual flame.' So, in a curious way, the flame of the candle, sometimes wavering, sometimes steady, could be likened to the soul – or the other way round.

There was an old country custom that the Christmas candle should be left burning through the night of Christmas Eve. This ritual, the old folk believed, would ensure prosperity in the new year ahead. This Christmas Eve pattern though was the exception to the candle rule in that generally you did not leave a candle burning in an empty room – not so much a sensible fire precaution but the belief in certain death to follow.

From the general to the specific and from the gloomy to the positive: I remember when Sonia and I faced the prospect of a difficult week-end, difficult to the extent that we were apprehensive. On the Friday evening I telephoned a psychic friend in Devon and she advised us to light a candle. It somehow helped us to concentrate and yet be more relaxed and interestingly the week-end passed without the problems we feared. Moreover in the long term that particular problem area improved. Our friend from Devon had told us 'The candle has a big advantage over negative things . . . it is a symbol of light.'

In dream experiences a candle can mean different things. It can indicate inner spiritual life or, in another context, a forthcoming birth. If extinguished the candle can mean either frustrated ambition or the death of a dear one. But most dream interpreters regard the candle as a very good omen promising an improvement in the dreamer's affairs. A strong steady flame in a dream predicts happiness or success – and sometimes both.

One person who sees candle burning as an important part of her life is Frances Shipp, who, with her husband Steven, runs Midnight Books from The Mount, Ascerton Road, Sidmouth, Devon. 'We are always burning candles,' she told me. 'Indeed our

◀ *FRANCES SHIPP, a few days before the birth of her son Gregory in June 1995. Frances and her husband Steve run Midnight Books from Sidmouth, South Devon. She says candle burning is an enjoyable part of their family life.*

two and a half year old Griselda loves to see candles burning and is always asking us to light them.

'For most people candles are usually used only at certain occasions, religious or ceremonial such as Halloween. They are also used in restaurants. But why? In all these instances to create atmosphere.

'I have been burning candles now for over fifteen years and have used them considerably during that time. Initially I started to use candle burning as an aid for meditation. If I needed to contemplate on something I found the candle flame would be a focal point for my concentration. There is a very soothing quality in the steady flicker of a candle flame. Sometimes I will play soft music as a background but more often than not I will rely on the stillness and quiet so that my mind is free only to focus on the flame. I find it very spiritually and emotionally cleansing – a way of relaxing and getting rid of troubles or worries as far as possible. There is a very uplifting feeling about such a simple pleasure as this, and also a very powerful one. I expect this powerful element is why candle burning is used for rituals.

'The colour of the candle can also be of importance. I find white a favourite of mine because of its purity and oneness. Green also is another I enjoy, which invokes the feeling of friendship. Orange and red are more vibrant and intense colours which I tend to use if I wish to think on a specific and difficult subject. I personally favour pastel colours and these days do not use dark colours such as black as I don't tend to identify with them. I use the colour that my mood requires at the particular time.

'I cannot imagine *not* burning candles. We tend to use them for lighting if we have friends over as their light is much kinder than the artificial variety which is far more intrusive and unnecessary for conversation.

'They are very important. I also have enjoyed making them in the past, quite a fiddly and sometimes messy business but with satisfying results. There is nothing like the homemade touch.'

HEALING
WITH CRYSTALS

MARY Tavy is an edge of the moor village. It sits above the river a mile from Peter Tavy. I came here on the last afternoon in November. Winter, in a way, suits the wildness of the moor, days when the heights of Dartmoor assume an extra dimension and drama.

I came to Mary Tavy to meet Josephine McCoy who lives at Oak Cottage near the war memorial. It was formerly a brace of miners' cottages.

A blonde Taurean subject with blue eyes, Josephine McCoy is a several-sided lady. She is a crystal therapist, a spiritual and natural healer and, when necessary, prescribes Bach Flower remedies. As her name suggests, she is married to an Irishman and her grandparents came from Ireland. 'I was born in Devonport,' she told me. 'I was born with a dimensional energy and taught by spirit and experiences in life, and was aware of psychic energies at the age of two. I was the seventh child but more like an only child because the others were a lot older. In a word I was a loner. As far as I know I'm the first healer in the family. Made my first steps as a healer around the age of seven . . . with animals. I have a very close affinity with domestic animals, cats and dogs . . . and the earth. Never knew my maternal grandmother but quickly established a spiritual relationship with her. I'd see her . . . this Edwardian lady and would visit her house when she lived there . . . one of those large houses on Plymouth Hoe.'

We talked in Josephine's healing room, a room filled with peace. Inside its four walls you are aware of all the powerful yet gentle healing work which has gone on here – that, anyway, was my response. Patients, struggling with the problems and pressures of modern living, must find it a spiritual oasis, and Josephine's calm underlines the tranquility. We were surrounded by dozens and dozens of crystals from various parts of the world. Quartz is the mineral with the widest range of crystal, including amethyst, agate and rock crystal. Alongside me were shelves lined with small brown bottles of flower remedies. These remedies take their name from Dr Edward Bach who lived and worked in the Oxfordshire countryside discovering and developing his healing flowers. They are prepared from the flowers of wild plants, bushes and trees. They are used, not directly, for physical complaints, but for the patient's worry, or apprehension, hopelessness or irritability, because these states of mind or mood hinder recovery of health and retard convalescence, and are generally accepted as primary causes of sickness and disease.

Dr Bach had great sensitivity both in mind and in body. When he held his hand over a flowering plant, or the flower in the palm of his hand, he could sense in himself the properties of that particular flower.

In thirty years of exploring the paranormal, this was my first interview with a crystal therapist. Josephine explained:

'Crystals have been used since the dawning of civilisation as an ancient healing art by old cultures, the Egyptians, Chinese and American Indians, and are frequently mentioned in the Bible. Crystals have many different healing properties and work when placed on the body, held or worn by the user. They work individually, resonating to one's personal energies healing the physical, emotional and spiritual, treating the whole person: body, mind and spirit.

'I work by tuning into the individual's energy field, intuitively selecting crystals for the person's needs which heal by working on the physical body, subtle body, and aura healing and cleansing on many levels. I use the crystal healing, complementing my natural and spiritual healing which together work with the whole energy system releasing old negative patterns and thoughts allowing self healing to be absorbed and positive energies to flow.'

She says she perceives a disturbance in the patient's aura and takes it from there focusing healing thoughts and energy through the crystal. 'I have diagnosed cancer . . . she had been brought here in spirit before she actually came!'

The crystals themselves are beautifully shaped mineral formations found in the seams and hollows of rocks, and healers maintain these very special stones have the ability to harmonise, transform and focus energy. In healing sessions the crystal is often placed on the affected part of the body, and in group meditation a large crystal is sometimes positioned in the centre of the circle enabling all the members of the group to concentrate on it.

Josephine McCoy is a perfect interviewee in that she talks quietly, slowly and clearly, intuitively knowing when to pause or push on with conversation. You sense those blue eyes miss very little, and she told me at the end of some healing sessions her eyes have changed to dark green.

CRYSTAL therapist and healer Josephine McCoy in her healing room at Oak Cottage. In thirty years of interviewing I have never visited a more peaceful, more powerful room. You feel something of all the good healing work which has gone on here – that, anyway, was my response.

THE BREAKFAST room at Oak Cottage which has been the scene of various supernatural happenings. Josephine's dogs have responded to the reappearance of long departed owners of the cottage in a friendly welcoming spirit.

She reminded me of my old friend the late Alan Nance, a celebrated healer from the Isles of Scilly. As soon as we shook hands you felt an immediate power. We talked for something like an hour and a half – our first face-to-face meeting – yet I felt I had known her for years. She has the ability to instil confidence – confidence in both senses of that word. Like one of her crystals she has a quiet energy.

Ours was a wide-ranging discussion. She is a convinced reincarnationist, and believes she has lived 'many lives, once as a Count in Austria, and I have made contact with our mutual friend Shirley Wallis in some of those earlier lives including a life in Egypt, another in Ireland, and in my work today I am helped by my spirit guide Running Water, an American Red Indian.'

I told her how when I had interviewed Shirley Wallis in regression, she – Shirley – had appeared to come over as a totally different personality. Josephine understood, quietly explaining: 'I have had experiences where my voice has changed, my physical appearance . . . and I was an Egyptian priestess. I also work with regressed healing, taking them back to earlier times. One lady went back to Atlantis.'

Crystals, of course, were used in old wirelesses and work today in quartz watches and clocks. 'UFOs have crystal power. I somehow know crystals are used for lift off and landing . . . I had a UFO visitation in September1993. It was about midnight and we had gone to bed . . . my husband was out like a light . . . but I was fully awake and aware of things, and suddenly someone had turned on this light inside me and inside the room and there was this tremendous build-up of spiritual and psychic energy and I was aware of other beings from outer space. I've had an alien guide for some years now. He's very tall like a column of golden and white light. There have been a number of UFO sightings over Dartmoor by various people. I find Dartmoor has a very strong energy and a healing quality . . . those ancient standing stones . . . and you have all these ley lines on the moor . . . one of them runs straight through this cottage. Coming to this cottage from Beacon Park, Plymouth, in 1990 was a spiritual move. A dream led me here, and when I walked up the path I knew this was it! It's not only changed my life, it's changed all our lives.

'Often at Oak Cottage I've seen previous owners, including a mining couple who lived here about one hundred and fifty years ago and my two collie dogs and cat see them too. The dogs will come bounding over to greet them . . . nothing frightening . . . all very friendly in fact.'

Finally a personal postscript. During the interview I decided to purchase a crystal from Josephine. Having chosen it, she then took the crystal and 'charged' it. For some time I have had problems with my left shoulder and back. By applying the crystal to the affected areas for a while on two successive evenings I discovered the problems had cleared. When I told Josephine a few weeks later, she said 'I had been giving you healing during the interview.'

Yes, it had been quite a November afternoon and as I write these words on a December afternoon the improvement in shoulder and back has been sustained.

DEJA VU

DEJA vu has its place in the *Collins English Dictionary* yet curiously appears only rarely inside the pages of paranormal books. I have to admit this is the first time I have tackled the subject. As it reads and sounds, déjà vu is French, meaning 'the experience of perceiving a new situation as if it had occurred before.'

Peter Underwood in his fine volume *Dictionary of the Supernatural*, published by Harrap in 1978, said:

'The feeling that it has all happened before, that you are in a place doing something which you have already done on a previous occasion; a common feeling that varies from a vague disquiet to a specific and detailed conviction. It has been supposed that déjà vu ('seen previously') is evidence for belief in reincarnation, but more likely it is the working of the subconscious mind triggered off on a particular course by an insignificant detail which escapes our conscious senses; and thus, reminding our unconscious mind of a similar incident or situation, persuading us that other details and happenings are also remembered. We are telling ourselves we were aware of what was about to take place, though in reality it was not until after the happening took place that we thought of it as a re-occurrence.'

We know a great deal more about ghosts than déjà vu, but, as with ghosts, the precise nature – or the triggering of such experiences remains a mystery. In due course, I believe we shall find more than one explanation about ghosts and that may well be the case here too. Given the diversity and peculiarity of men and women how could it be otherwise?

◀ *AUTHOR and painter Ken Duxbury had a very strange experience . . .*

I recall a young Cornish woman telling me how her husband serving in the army, was taken ill during his national service. She and her parents went to visit him in a clinic in a part of the United Kingdom which neither she nor her parents had visited before.

'I was doing the map-reading on this journey,' she recalled. 'Father was driving and suddenly we found ourselves on a stretch of road about three miles from the clinic and I instinctively knew I'd been here before. It was so eerie and so accurate . . . I even knew how the clinic would look, its entrance and so on, a mile or so before it came into sight . . . very strange but very true. It was all so real . . . as if I had been there in a previous life.'

Sonia, my wife, says on several occasions she has known 'instinctively and immediately I've been here *before* though I have had no recollection as to how or why. It's just the certain feeling that you know this place.'

Hilary Rogers, who lives near Truro, told me: 'I dreamt about a meeting with this solicitor; we had an appointment and were scheduled to sign some legal documents. But we didn't sign them at the arranged interview. Instead the solicitor said, "You can take these papers home and read them first . . ." and suddenly I realized I had had this very same conversation in the dream, the real life experience following the precise procedure of the earlier dream.'

Two writers who know all about the significance of dreams are Julia and Derek Parker. In their beautifully illustrated book, *Dreaming*, published by Mitchell Beazley in 1985, they wrote:

'One of the most refreshing and exhilarating dream experiences we can have is of travelling to some distant land, and waking with such vivid memories of it that we feel we have actually been there. It has sometimes been claimed that the feeling of déjà vu, of "I have been here before", stems from just such an experience, and there are records of people having described very accurately places which they have never visited, except in dreams.'

Perhaps the last words on this subject should come from an experience here in Cornwall. Ken Duxbury is an old friend of mine. He is the author of a dozen books and a gifted water colour artist. Ken, by the way, is a perceptive and very down-to-earth character, certainly not the kind of man to mistake imagination for reality. Here is the story he told me.

'Some years ago my wife was engaged in editing books for a publisher in London and she decided to purchase a dictating machine to reduce the amount of writing involved. This was in the early days of tape-recording before the small and technically sophisticated units we now know were available. Prices of such units were high so she perused Exchange and Mart for a serviceable second-hand bargain.

'Eventually a suitable advert appeared to which she replied. In due course the unit arrived by courier and I was sitting reading in our lounge when she took delivery of the heavy and well-wrapped cardboard box. She brought it to the table, removed it from the box and started to fit the separate microphone on to its stand before plugging into the mains. I glanced across . . .

"Oh!" I said, "that brings back memories. It's exactly like the one I used for many years – quite an old friend in fact." I went over to the table and took a closer look. 'Ah no,' I added. 'Mine had slightly different tape reels, they were open to view whereas these are enclosed . . . and another difference, mine had a red scale and pointer which indicated the amount to tape left on the reel is black. Otherwise it is identical." With which I returned to my reading.

'Moments later I began to doubt my sanity. Never in my life have I owned or used such a machine or anything like it. But the feeling of recognition was too powerful to shrug off. Indeed I recognised the name of the instrument – Stenorette – and tried hard to focus and regain a strong impression, to extend that moment of recognition and perhaps get some idea of my environ at the time I had used the Stenorette. But like a dream, the more I tried the more the impression faded.

'Now I am aware of psychometry in others – it is the faculty of divining from physical contact with an object some qualities of a person who had previously been in contact with the object. Personally I had no experience of such a thing. But this was strangely different, for I had not 'tapped' the persona and memory of the previous owner of this machine, but that of some other person who had used an instrument similar but not identical to it. A sort of psychic phenomenon by proxy as it were! Not an earth-shattering experience it's true, but that sense of sharing just for one moment the actual persona of another human being was so powerful that it has remained with me over the years.

'Certainly this was nothing to do with reincarnation for such instruments were not invented before I was born into this life. But I knew with absolute certainty that for that one moment I shared the actual living experience of some other, and totally unknown, person, and it has made me reflect on the exact nature of consciousness. Are we in some way all sharing a sort of Cosmic awareness which just occasionally gets its lines crossed?'

STRANGE HAPPENINGS

A while back my cricket friend Jack Burrell of Bristol recalled his only experience of anything like the supernatural. 'This concerns a hit and run raid on the Aeroplane Works at Yate, which is about ten miles north of Bristol. I worked for that firm for a few weeks and in 1950 had a look at the mass grave in Yate Churchyard. Among the names were three men whom I had known in my time there. Over twenty years later I was passing near with a friend and asked her if she knew of the grave. She did not, so we stopped and had a look at it. To my amazement the three names of those three men were not there! And I am certain the names were not blocked out through burial elsewhere.'

I put Jack's baffling case to psychical researcher Shirley Wallis who lives near Plymouth, and these were her findings. 'I tuned in to all three men,' she wrote in her report, 'and it seems two of the men were working at the time of the raid. One died two years after the raid which had exacerbated a physical condition. The second man was injured in the raid but again he died a few years later as a result of injuries. The third man seems the odd one. He died of other causes and doesn't seem to have been working on the premises at the time of the raid.

'Tremendous confusion arose as remains were unidentifiable and lists of who was on duty lost. There was naturally a tremendous shock wave continuously active on etheric levels which disturbed the area and still does to this day. I feel the whole incident is veiled in some secrecy.

'At the time that Jack Burrell saw the names on the memorial the three were dead. Jack was tuning in to the incident and the three people he knew, on unconscious levels. He quite clearly *saw* the names – it was not an illusion, because he was being given information about his colleagues having died.

'I would like to assure Jack Burrell that he was not deluded over this incident, if we are to try and use three dimensional language to explain fourth dimensional experiences. The conditioning of the brain, (like programmes in a computer), cannot find the logical explanation if it has not been programmed to do so. Especially, if a person uses the left-hand part of the brain – logical, verbal, and analytical – which codes memory in *linguistic* description – while the right-hand hemisphere codes memory *in images*. The right specialises in the understanding of patterns and intuition.

'We must try to be aware that violent events on the surface of this planet have a long lasting effect of disturbing the energy field in the particular area of the event. People who are sensitive (using their right-hand brain coding) can feel this more than others. Some feel a sense of atmosphere, knowing that there is something different about a place or area, while very left-hand brain people 'sense' something but dismiss it through their left-hand coding which cannot identify – and they are inclined to voice words like "poppycock" or "delusion" or "you're losing your marbles!" All quite understandable, but usually a conclusion reached out of fear.

'As for Jack returning to the memorial after twenty years had elapsed . . . no names. After a good number of years the original energy effect loses its impact and rearranges itself, *although the image is still there* but lessened, especially if new buildings, new people, new energies etc impinge on the place. The second visit, twenty years later, did not open the window on the message – no need anyway – the message had been delivered and received!'

Earlier Harry Cleverly expressed the view that most ghosts are friendly characters – and I agree but some paranormal activity is of a violent nature, notably when a poltergeist is at work.

In my records I have accounts of a saucepan of water on a stove being thrown violently and water streaming all over the floor, a chair crashing into a sitting room fender, a mat being lifted from the floor, crockery and ornaments flying around a room.

These 'rattling ghosts' produce all kind of disturbances, but they are not really regarded as 'ghosts' at all. *The Directory of Possibilities,*

SHIRLEY WALLIS, who lives at Plymstock, Plymouth, operates in various spiritual fields. She is a consultant for astrology, relaxation, meditation and healing.

edited by Colin Wilson and John Grant, refers to poltergeists as 'manifestations of unconscious mental disturbance, usually in children and teenagers . . .' How objects fly through the air remains a mystery, but there is no doubt they do – and sometimes very heavy objects. At present the explanation is unknown to science, but some of us believe it may have something to do with energy and 'the darker side of the human mind.'

One night in November 1995 Brenda Gracey was suddenly awakened by a mighty crash at her Minehead home. It sounded like someone coming in through the window, but instead she found a very solid oak dresser had been turned upside down. There were three puzzling things. First, the dressing table was originally wedged between two wardrobes – now she found it in the middle of the floor and upside down. Curiously a large mirror and other ornaments which were on it were completely undamaged. And thirdly when she called the police they could find no evidence of any forced entry and recorded the case as 'unexplained.'

But one man who had an explanation was parapsychologist Bill Harrison of Wedmore. He believed the bedroom was inhabited by the spirit of a Victorian miner who in his earthly life lived in an adjacent but hidden attic room.

Mr Harrison, speaking to the *Western Daily Press* said: 'He was about 5ft 7in tall, of stocky build with dark hair and his name was Jack Roberts or Robertson. He used to be a miner, but went on to work with horses. He passed away in 1896 due to breathing problems and some sort of head injury, but the cause of death was unclear. He was what I would call a lost soul. He was present to remind people of an anniversary, probably his death, and to make sure he wasn't forgotten. I spoke to him and reassured him and he has not reappeared since, much to the delight of Brenda who was somewhat scared to find a ghost wandering about her bedroom.'

Now to a different kind of strange happening.

In early December 1995 I received this report from a lady who works in the City of Truro: 'I drive a fairly beaten-up red Peugeot van, and whilst driving to work one morning I was slowing down approaching the dual carriageway when my whole surroundings changed. I was sitting in a very plush comfortable heavily padded seat behind a leather steering wheel, looking at a padded dashboard and elaborate instrument panel. Everything was dark grey and the bonnet of the car a metallic dark grey. The feeling was of a brand new large saloon, the make of which I have no idea. The whole experience lasted only seconds but was very real. I never spend time thinking about cars. I have no interest in them, so, no thought transference.'

ANIMALS AND THE PARANORMAL

MY active membership of the International League for the Protection of Horses reflects a deep interest in equine welfare. The ILPH is, in fact, the largest equine welfare charity in the world, and exists for global protection and rehabilitation of equines. I recommend all lovers of horses, ponies and donkeys to support it or, better still, become members.

As a boy I liked to think animals, when they died, went on to another better place. That was the wishful thinking of youth, but, as a result of researching into the paranormal, I came to the view that animals – or some animals – *do* go beyond the thing we call death. The sighting of so many animal phantoms adds weight to that view, and two totally different men, whom I respected greatly in their lifetimes, both believed animals had an afterlife: Tony Polden, a highly rated Irish veterinary surgeon who did great work here in North Cornwall, and Alan Nance, Spiritualist and spiritual healer.

Occasionally one comes across a case which combines animal and human ghosts. Such a case came to me from Bill Picard of Clodgy Moor, Paul, near Penzance:

'One evening, just as it was getting dark in the September of 1948, I was walking through Kerris and had just come to the angle of the garden wall of the old manor house, when I noticed a figure on horseback ambling across the space in front of the house towards the entrance to the lane out of the village. There had been rain earlier and the muddy lane and the farmyard space had many puddles, which I was intent on avoiding; so I took my eyes off the horseman for a moment to see where I was treading and on looking up again I was very surprised to see he had vanished! Yet I could not see how he could have got out of the space ahead of me in the time I glanced away. I also remembered thinking there was something odd about his dress: he had on a long overcoat, and what looked like a flat fur hat on his head, and gaiters on his legs. But as it was only three years after the war, a lot of farm labourers were wearing old army or airforce coats and other military garments, so the long overcoat I supposed was ex-army, and did not attach much importance to the strangeness of the figure's clothing, and soon forgot the puzzle of how had he vanished while I apparently had only looked away for a second or so to avoid a puddle! Anyway, I forgot all about the incident.

'Then one evening, again walking through Kerris, which by then I must have done many times, on another September, and this time in 1968, I had a repeat of the incident. I had just reached the same spot and was looking across the open space towards the entrance to the lane, when I saw the same figure; and the moment I saw the horseman I remembered I had seen the exact same figure moving across the place years before. The moment I saw it this time I felt a sensation up the back of my neck, and a sudden feeling of coldness, as I realized this had all happened before. This time I never took my eyes off the figure, and noted that what I took the first time for an ex-army greatcoat, was actually slightly different; it was pulled in at the waist and had wider lapels, though the flat fur hat and gaiters was as I remembered them. But this time I had the impression the horse was being led by someone, while the rider sat slightly bowed with his hands apparently just resting on the front of the saddle. At the same time I felt a kind of sadness come over me, and then I realized the horse's hooves were making no sound on the surface of the road, which since the first time had now been macadamed or surfaced. As I watched, when the figures reached the entrance to the lane, they simply were suddenly not there: one moment I could see them and then they had vanished. This time of course I was sure I had seen a ghost that first time as well: there was no question of the horseman turning down any side entrances or through any gateways.

'After this second sighting I naturally asked around, when the opportunity came up in conversation; but in the Kerris area they all firmly said they knew nothing about it, though some told me of incidents when they had heard galloping horses, and even the sound of angry voices around the village when there was no one there; but no one admitted to seeing anything. Then several years later, my Principal at the Art School in Penzance, Mr Tudor, was on holiday in Wales, when he chanced to get talking to two strangers in a pub, who told him how they had been camping down in Cornwall, and had spent a night at Kerris, which had upset and frightened them; so much so that the wife said she would not come to Cornwall again. It seems they were camping in a field by the Chapel, when they awoke in the night hearing a commotion and the sound of galloping horses coming across the field in the darkness and right at their tent, the wife I understand threw herself across her child, while the husband was trying to get out of the tent to divert the horses. At the time, he was quite sure that the animals must have got into the field, though he could not see anything in the darkness. But it was as though 'a something, perhaps like a wind,' simply passed right through the tent, and then silence. In the morning they couldn't leave quickly enough, it had frightened them so much. Mr Tudor was surprised to be told about this incident, quite spontaneously, by strangers who only knew he came from Cornwall, but having heard of my experience he then told them about the horseman.

'Mrs Elizabeth Sparrow of nearby Red House, has made quite a study of Kerris Manor's history, and has an idea that a Col Oxenham of the local militia in the early part of the last century, might be the figure I saw, in view of the apparent military looking greatcoat. She also thinks that the figure and the sound of horses and voices may be a kind of "psychic replay" of some encounter between the local smugglers and the militia, as it appears the lane through Kerris was a smugglers way.'

Two interesting dog accounts have come to me from Ann Jennings who lives at Trevellas, St Agnes:

'February 3 1995 was sunny with the crisp air that you experience in the winter months. Eric, my beloved Great Dane, and I had enjoyed a walk along the beach that morning, stopping now and again to enjoy a paddle in the very cold sea water. Eric always enjoyed these walks and even though he was now an old man and his pace had slowed right down, he always enjoyed looking at the sea.

'After lunch a friend had rung and asked if I would like to meet up with her and her dogs to walk over the fields behind my cottage. Eric and I set off and he was more than pleased to meet his friends.

'After a short while my friend grabbed my arm and told me to look at Eric. He was stood alone in the field looking up into the sky, his ears straining forward and he had the most wonderful look on his face. We could not see nor hear anything. His tail began to wag from side to side. My walking partner remarked on how very beautiful he looked. He was so handsome and moved like a lion, his shoulders rolling. As we stood looking at this extraordinary sight he moved and turned for home walking more quickly than he had done for months.

'On arrival he went to his bed, he then came to fetch me out of the kitchen and, as on so many previous occasions, we lay down together. I could sense a difference in him, he was very calm and peaceful, stretched out with his head on a comfy blanket. Every time I went to rise he restrained me with his large front leg. I had no idea that I only had a short time left with him. After a couple of hours he looked up at me, gave a deep sigh and died. He was so fit and healthy it didn't seem possible that he had gone.

'I truly believe that his brother Edgar, who had died two years earlier, had called him to say it was his time. There is no other explanation for the way he behaved.'

Ann Jennings's second account concerns a relatively rare experience: a shared sighting:

'Six months after the death of Kahn, another of my Danes, my son Frank, who is in his early twenties, and I were sat watching television. Frank suddenly shouted out "Mother, quick quick look at the door". There stood Kahn, he was looking around the door and sucking in his lips as he did when he wanted to go out. We could see his head, left shoulder and leg. This vision lasted for about 30-40 seconds. I rushed into the next room to make sure it wasn't one of the other dogs but they were all sound asleep.'

Two more canine reports: this time from Victor Dunstan, a Welsh businessman and writer in Cardiff.

KAHN who has reappeared in very life-like form. He has been seen by his ▶
owner and her son.

57

'Many years ago, I had a Boxer dog that remained a puppy all her life. One morning we heard very plaintive howling and we thought the dog might be in pain. We hurried out to find her standing over a letter that had just been delivered. When we opened the letter, we found that it contained news that a good friend of ours had drowned in tragic circumstances. It was the only time the dog ever howled!

'On another occasion the actress Ann Todd saw an advertisement in the *Sunday Times* for my *Virgin Mary* book and she asked me to advise on a script she was planning called *Talitha*. It was a fantasy about the grandmother of Jesus. During one of my visits she told me how she was aware of the presence of Whisky, a dog that had died some years before. She was so convinced that she'd heard him bark and heard his footsteps in the hall that she wrote about it in her autobiography. When Judy Garland visited Ann in London during Whisky's lifetime, Judy used to cuddle him and sing Over the Rainbow to him. After Whisky died, whenever she played Judy singing that song, Ann said she felt the presence of Whisky. Ann died a while ago – I hope she found Whisky somewhere out there.'

The reaction of animals to a supernatural situation can be very revealing – confirmation that something is not quite of this world?

I had been lunching with Nicholas and Frances Kendall at their lovely home Pelyn high above Lostwithiel and during the meal conversation turned to ghosts. Later they drove me along a minor road which slopes down from the hamlet of Sweetshouse to the main A390, fringed by Redmoor on one side with a distant view of Restormel Castle on the other. They told me how late one pre-war afternoon on this lonely stretch of road Jill Kendall, a sister of Nicholas's, was riding home from a day's hunting.

'Jill was riding a horse, Gary Owen, an Irish hunter, an animal of very quiet temperament. Walking along the road, going in the same direction were two women. The horse suddenly and uncharacteristically became excitable, and Jill had the utmost difficulty in getting Gary Owen past the two women. Once past, however, she turned around to apologise . . . they'd vanished! She came back to Pelyn in a great state, explaining they couldn't have simply disappeared . . . there was no gateway through which they could have slipped. She was convinced she'd seen two ghosts. One unusual thing Jill had noticed was that both women were wearing white

stockings – this was in the 1930s when such things were unfash-
ionable – could they have been from a century earlier, when stockings weren't dyed?'

It was, I think, a large flock of birds on Davidstow Moor that first
made me think about telepathy. There were dozens and dozens of
them and yet they rose as one and went away in the direction of
Rough Tor. It was a dramatic sight. No call required, the leading
bird thought about the direction – and telepathy did the rest.

Soon after that we became the owners of a beautiful collie cross
called Rex. This dog and I established a great rapport. In due
course, he travelled everywhere with me. We even watched cricket
together on the county ground at Bristol. If a day went well, Rex
understood it and shared it – he understood other days too. When

*POLLY, a much loved pet owned by Rosemarie Hawkins of Barnstaple.
Though the dog eventually died of cancer, Rosemarie is convinced Polly
derived enormous benefit from spiritual healing. The good response of sick
animals to healing dents the cynical view of mind over matter and confirms
the sensitivity of many members of the animal kingdom.*

he died, the Cornish author Derek Tangye wrote of Rex: 'He shared your struggles and your triumphs'. Rex came with me to a number of haunted locations, and I noted and valued his reaction. We once visited a property where a murder had been committed. I found it a perfectly normal place – no hint of a bloody past, it was like a house exorcised – and Rex agreed: no canine agitation. Rex came with me on several occasions to haunted St Nectan's near Tintagel. There have been many sightings of ghostly monk figures in grey in this lovely wooded glen, but Rex never showed a trace of apprehension which confirmed the opinion of people I had interviewed: the monks are friendly spirits.

Near his earthly end, Rex became rather deaf, but deafness did not destroy our unspoken communication. I thought of Rex and that fact when I read a sentence by Tom Lethbridge in his magnificent book *The Power of the Pendulum*: 'Whether telepathy is conveyed by ultrasonic sound I very much doubt, for sound is relatively slow as you can see if you watch a man hammering in a post on the opposite side of a valley.'

Finally back to horses and their sensitivity which probably explains why so many of them appear in so many cases.

I talked with Maggie Ginger who lives at Kelland Cross, Lapford near Crediton. Maggie, a Torquay girl, is a freelance graphic designer – responsible for this Bossiney cover and many others over the years. She knows how to capture the essence of a book in its cover and understands the importance of creative marketing. She also works with her husband Les in their signwriting business.

An accomplished horsewoman with a special interest in dressage, Maggie Ginger has owned and kept horses all her life.

'The relationship between horse and human has enabled us to gain a fuller insight into their behaviour, sensitivity and individual characteristics' she explained. 'For his part the horse appears to have the ability to sum up his human counterpart fairly rapidly, and often quicker than anticipated as many a non-rider mounted for the first time will be well aware!

'But with the highly trained dressage horse and rider the harmony between the two is evident and the strong, powerful equine and often diminutive female rider is transformed into a display of almost invisible aids and a near telepathic union exist between

MAGGIE GINGER at home with her horse Mikado, whom she bred, and her dog Biggles. Maggie has a great love of animals – and some interesting thoughts on the sensitivity of horses in particular.

horse and rider. This, to me, exhibits the height of channelled sensitivity that man can achieve in harmony with his mount. It is not strange then that there are many occasions when a horse's reactions to 'imaginary' objects causing snorting and excitability, or transfixed alert stare at some undetected item on the horizon leave us less perceptive mortals in bewilderment.

'There is one story which I would like to relate concerning the death of my friend's dearly loved horse 'Ben'. She had owned him from weaning at six months of age and he and his donkey companion grazed happily together until at the age of twenty-three years Ben died. He was buried in the field in a spot not usually frequented by animals, but now when my friend looks across the field she often finds the donkey has chosen to stand directly over the burial spot as if drawn to that particular location.

'A strange experience happened to the wife of a colleague of mine at Killerton Horse Trials. His wife, when walking in the grounds, saw people in period costume at what appeared to be a fete of some kind. The husband could not see this vision but the wife was convinced, so much so that they went to the house and related the experience. The person in attendance confirmed that what had been seen had been reported on various occasions before.

'Getting back specifically to horses I heard of a fascinating case recently. It happened some years ago when two women riding in the vicinity of Hunter's Tor, Lustleigh Cleave came across a dozen men on horseback . . . there were others on foot and some greyhounds . . . quite a contingent. The odd thing is all the men were dressed in medieval costume . . . actors on location for a film, they thought. Very curious about this contingent, the two women followed them until the group of strange riders, horses, walkers and greyhounds were hidden by a stone wall, and when the two modern women riders rode past the wall the medieval group had disappeared into thin air, and when they searched neither woman could find any hoofprints in the soft ground . . . only those of their own horses.'

QUEEN Elizabeth II, who for many years has been convinced of the ▶ *healing quality of homeopathy, is reputed to have been treated for a shoulder injury by spiritual healer Kay Kiernan. Her Majesty is a typical Taurus subject in that she enjoys country life, horses and dogs. She has an expert's eye for horses and it is no coincidence that she is so successful as a racehorse owner.*

DISAPPEARANCES

NOT all disappearances are strictly supernatural in nature, but a great many of them are deep mysteries. It is an uncomfortable fact that some people seemingly vanish from life. One of the most sensational vanishing acts was that of Victor Grayson, a Labour politician who was an eloquent spokesman on matters of social injustice.

In 1920 Grayson took the night train from Liverpool to Hull. When the train arrived at its destination he was not aboard. He had simply disappeared into thin air, and nobody came up with a really feasible explanation for the Socialist's disappearance.

Two people believed they later saw Victor Grayson. In 1932 a political colleague, G A Murray, was convinced he had seen Grayson from the top of a London bus, and another ex-colleague reckoned he had spotted Grayson on the London underground. He was accompanied by a lady who called him 'Vic' and when they left the train near the Houses of Parliament, the man said with a laugh: 'Here's the old firm!'

Outside these sightings, there were further claims of people seeing him in Australia, one as late as 1957 when Victor Grayson would have been seventy five years old. If the sightings in the United Kingdom were genuine it is an incredible fact that he remained hidden or under another identity for so long. If however the London sightings were a mistake, then something very odd must have happened on that night train in 1920 between Liverpool and Hull. Whichever way we look at his end, it remains a baffling mystery.

An earlier disappearance concerned Benjamin Bathurst who was the British envoy to Vienna during the Napoleonic Wars. In 1809 on a journey from Vienna via Berlin to Hamburg, following a carefully planned route to avoid French troops, Benjamin Bathurst stopped at a small town called Perleberg to change his coach horses. The envoy went behind the coach and was never seen again. It were as if the very earth had opened up and swallowed him.

The Bathurst family spent a great deal of money, time and energy trying to trace what actually happened. The British government offered a reward of £1,000 and the Bathursts offered a matching reward – sizeable sums of money in those days. In the spring of 1810, the young Mrs Bathurst went to Perleberg and throughout Germany and France, travelling with a passport obtained from Napoleon himself. Her last communication from her husband had been on a dirty scrap of paper. In it Benjamin Bathurst expressed fear about his future and made sinister reference to a certain Comte d'Entraigues. In Europe Mrs Bathurst heard various explanations about her husband's disappearance or demise: he had escaped from Germany but had drowned in the Baltic, he had been killed by a servant, he had been imprisoned at Magdelburg.

On her return to England Mrs Bathurst received a visit from Comte d'Entraigues. She treated this with natural caution – wise caution for he proved to be a double agent. He told Mrs Bathurst her husband had indeed been taken to Magdelburg Prison. She insisted on proof and, perhaps to her surprise, he promised such proof. But no proof emerged. Only a few days later Comte d'Entraigues and his wife – who was reputed to know all his secrets – emerged from their London residence when a recently appointed French servant plunged a dagger into her breast. She died there in the street. The count raced back to his room for his pistols. Two shots were heard and the count and the French servant were found dead.

After this triple killing and high drama, no further clues emerged and Mrs Bathurst reconciled herself to the fact that her husband had died in Europe. His mother never gave up hope. But Benjamin Bathurst was never seen again - and no body was ever found. A German writer of the time reflected 'The disappearance of the English ambassador seems like magic.'

Such disappearances remind us fact is frequently stranger than fiction. In London alone in an average week it is calculated that ten people vanish and are seemingly lost for ever.

Over the years explanations have varied. Once upon a time such events were thought to be the work of the Devil. Later it was said abductions were made by the fairies or the 'little people' and, more recently, there has been talk of kidnappings by UFOs.

Here in the Westcountry Genette Tate, the Devon schoolgirl, remains our big unsolved mystery, and I have heard of two separate cases of people going out of their homes – and never coming back.

One of the most incredible disappearances of all time related to Lord Lucan who allegedly battered to death his children's nanny, Sandra Rivett, believing her to be his wife Veronica. This happened in Lower Belgrave Street, London and his abandoned car was found in Sussex.

Despite intense enquiries both in Britain and overseas Lord Lucan remains a missing person on police files. But on Monday November 6 1995 came a startling press interview in the *Western Morning News*. Joanna Webber of Talaton, near Honiton, Devon, told Chris Carson how she believed she had had lunch with the missing Lord in South Africa in 1975. She said he had undergone plastic surgery and his hair was dyed grey to make him look older.

Mrs Webber recalled: 'My husband John was convinced it was Lord Lucan but there was this strange loyalty to the man. It is only now, nearing the 21st anniversary of his disappearance, with all the speculation going on, and the fact that my husband died four years ago, that I have felt able to speak about it.'

Mrs Webber said she met the man she believes was Lord Lucan when she and her husband invited some friends to lunch and he was in the party.

'When they arrived the supposed Lord Lucan was with them, but was not introduced as such, but, I believe, just as a friend. I felt he was being paraded in front of us to see what our reaction would be. It was all a bit awkward. He was a really charming man but there was something rather strange about him.'

One man who has some thoughts and theories on disappearances is the cricket historian Jack Burrell of Bristol.

'Disappearances are always interesting and during World War 11 there were examples of members of the rank and file disappearing. I issued a chap with a weekend pass and he did not come back and I was in that unit for another year but he never reappeared. How they managed, in view of rationing, I do not know and cannot see how they could have left the country. The war also did away, to a large extent, with tramps as they had to take up a more settled way of life in view of rationing. Rationing was the biggest problem for those who disappeared. What did these people do with themselves all the time they were on the run? How did they get a job and what of the neighbours? People with dear ones away in the forces would have had rather mixed feelings about these characters.

'I came across a chap who was on the run from late 1942 until the spring of 1944. He lived in a tough part of the east end of London and among the sort who might have covered for him. Another interesting example was a soldier from Hamilton in Scotland. He was determined not to serve and would bunk as soon as he had finished his period of detention. Oddly I got on very well with him

A GERMAN bomber shot down on Dartmoor during the last war. As Jack Burrell recalls in this chapter the war years saw a surprising number of disappearances – surprising because one feels bound to ask 'Where did such people go?'

when I was his escort. He once said "Dinna argue with him, he's an expert on cricket and reads books about it . . ." In 1943 he went on leave from Westbury, Wiltshire and he, of course, did not come back. This Scot was connected with horse racing, and I believe there were a few meetings during the war and they reckoned he could make enough money at each meeting to last him a while.

'Another thing, of course, about wartime disappearances was that it would have been very difficult to disappear . . . and where does one go in England? In rural areas people would soon ask questions. I suppose the eastender stood the best chance, but probably someone gave him away in the end.

'I can just remember the Rouse case in 1931. Rouse had too many financial commitments through women and found that the only way out was to make it appear as if he was dead. He chatted with a tramp and found out that he had not a relation in the world. Rouse offered to give him a lift northwards from London. He then said there was a fault with the engine and asked the tramp to have a look at it with him. As the tramp leaned over the engine Rouse knocked him out, set the car alight and threw his body into the flames. With less knowledge of forensic matters then, he might have got away with it but for one thing which made all the difference. It was Guy Fawkes night, and as he walked away from the wreckage two people, coming from a Guy Fawkes night party, spotted him in view of it being brighter.

'Kilvert is usually good for an account on matters such as a disappearance. Here is something he wrote: "Clyro, Radnorshire 17th March 1872. Went into Wall's House after chapel and had some talk with him on the Tichborne case. He instanced the loss and return of Charles James Phillips of Wye Cliff who was believed to be dead and buried in Australia. He was advertised for. The advertisement was answered by an announcement from Australia that Charles James Phillips had died and was buried there. His family sent out an agent to make enquiries. The agent was satisfied of the death and burial of the person in question. Yet the young man returned in rags and accosted his aunt in Hereford streets. She disowned him. Yet he proved his identity and proved that he had never been to Australia."'

MYSTERIOUS
LOCATIONS

THE past is mysterious. Why? I remember putting that question to my old tutor Edmund Sedding. He reasoned the fascination of the past lay largely on one fact – much of it is *lost*. Edmund, a gifted product of Cambridge University, had a second interesting theory. He maintained historians learn as much about a nation's development through studying its folklore as reading the pages of factual history books.

Years later I discussed the same question with the painter and writer Charles Simpson. We were talking about it in relation to Cornwall and her past. 'There is an atmosphere of age in Cornwall,' he said. 'The early history of man still seems to brood over the Cornish moors and hills.' He once wrote of the Penwith landscape: 'The land has a countenance whose smiles only intensify its gloom and if there is laughter on the hills it is hollow as the cackle of an aged man.' Like Edmund Sedding, Charles believed the old folk wove weird and wonderful stories around ancient features on the moors which made the countryside alive and vital.

You cannot move around the Westcountry and not be aware of earlier times. If, for example, a Dorset journey takes me to Shaftesbury I invariably think of Shaftesbury Abbey in its heyday – now there are only ruins. Local tradition has it a certain monk buried the abbey's treasure hereabouts but took the precise location to his grave. They say his ghost walks among the ruins and one witness swore the phantom monk was walking on his knees. I doubt it. Far more likely the ground level has been raised since his earthly days, for ghosts, as a general rule, stick to their old ways.

There is a school of thought which believes events of the past make their impression on the atmosphere – and those impressions stay. We sometimes say certain people 'create an atmosphere' by their attitude – they may be warm and friendly or aggressive and hostile – but places have a more profound, more permanent atmosphere when sensitive people visit them.

Moreover I am not just thinking of paranormal subjects or mysterious locations. I happen to be a very keen cricketer and loyal member of Gloucestershire County Cricket Club, and invariably come to the county ground at Bristol with a sense of awe. It's all to do with Gloucestershire's glorious past: Dr W G Grace, the father of the modern game who performed such great deeds here, Gilbert Jessop, legendary hitter, Bev Lyon, the bold unconventional captain, the majestic batting of Walter Hammond, the guile of Charlie Parker's bowling and the cavalier stroke play of Charles Barnett. John Arlott felt this aura when he wrote: 'I must confess that I always approach the Gloucestershire ground at Bristol with a higher expectation of memorable cricket than I feel at any other ground. The entire history of Gloucestershire cricket is full, for me, of the names of men who played in the epic manner.'

But back to mysterious locations: in this, the late twentieth century large areas of our land may be criss-crossed by motorways yet surprisingly there remain lonely and mysterious places and, at this point on our journey, I suggest we explore just four of them.

Cadbury Castle

King Arthur remains a major mystery. Did he reign in reality or in legend? Some of us think the Once and Future King reigned in both, and more and more people now see him as an historical probability.

Rosemary Clinch in *King Arthur in Somerset*, first published by Bossiney in 1987, and still in print, has written: '. . . an impressive hill crowned by a hillfort, one of the finest in the county. It is South Cadbury Castle, the tantalising dream of Arthur's Court – Camelot.

'There is no doubting the kingly appearance of this ancient hill, five hundred feet in height, for the massive ramparts of the Iron-Age hillfort heave themselves above the thickly wooded slopes. They dominate the little village of South Cadbury below, where near the church we find the rough stoney path of Arthur's Lane with its scattered cowpats. Here we begin our gradual climb, the lane giving way to a more uneven track, soft with the mulch of mud and leaves. Thick, overhanging trees on either side lean their trunks curiously inwards from their banks as if drawn magnetically together by some hidden force. High above, their boughs inter-mingle to form dark green vaulting and an impression of some grand primeval aisle. Eventually the trees open, revealing the large grassy plateau of the hill surrounded by an undulating rampart and breath-taking view.'

In supernatural investigations I try to keep clear of legendary associations. In the case of Arthur, this is impossible. For the moment there is no hard evidence of his reality – and we may

CADBURY: a location which encourages curiosity and speculation. In **King Arthur in the West** *Felicity Young has written: 'Legends of Arthur abound here-abouts which can only strengthen the feeling that there is no smoke without fire.'*

never get the required proof. But there is no doubt Arthur and his knights have been seen here in ghostly form, and eyewitnesses claim to have glimpsed the King's phantom figure among the ruins of Tintagel Castle in North Cornwall.

All of which brings us to this crucial question: 'Can there be such a thing as the ghost of a legend?' Personally I think not. If Arthur's ghost has been seen then surely we must assume he once lived.

We must remember too there have been sightings of 'a radiant female phantom' in the vicinity of Glastonbury Tor – some say she is Guinevere. So maybe the Court of Camelot did belong to genuine history, and Cadbury, as a place, encourages us to speculate.

'There is not much to see here,' reflected one travel writer. He was probably a man of little imagination because you cannot come to Cadbury and not be curious about the whole Arthurian scene. Only a powerful theme answering some deep sense of national character – and characters – could have been sustained for so long and so diversely. Standing here at Cadbury you firmly believe the Arthurian tales will continue to flourish: future writers and film makers cherishing the central themes and yet remoulding them, reshaping them to meet the requirements of a new age.

That is at the heart of Arthur's mystery and magic.

Avebury

The ancient stones of Avebury do various things. Above all, they provoke questions.

Who brought them here? How did they get here – sledges or rollers? How many men were crippled or killed by moving them? They are, of course, questions without answer. Despite the research and the analysis, all we have is conjecture and surmise.

Older than Stonehenge, today relatively little of the original Avebury splendour remains. Sadly, many of the old stones were smashed into pieces, used for building purposes locally in the 1600s and 1700s.

If we take complexity and size as criteria, then these earthworks and related stone structures are undoubtedly the most impressive monuments of their time in the whole of Great Britain.

Despite those missing stones, Avebury retains a certain nobility. The stones remind me of the sculptures of Dame Barbara

STANDING stones at Avebury.

Hepworth. They watch us silently. If only they could speak, they would have incredible stories to tell.

Fires crimsoning the sky, people dancing, drums beating, effigies burning: those are only some of the images in the eye of our imagination.

The fires are out and the stones cannot speak or could we be wrong? Maybe the bones of this ancient landscape are not speechless – that is provided we are humble and receptive.

Avebury is part of the great St Michael ley line. The basis of the ley line system is very simple – that sites of ancient importance *align*. On ley line sites one invariably experiences a heightened sense of well-being – as in the case of spiritual healing. Tom Lethbridge once said '. . . there are other realms of reality beyond our world . . . and forms of energy we do not even begin to understand.' At Avebury you feel you are on the edge of another realm and in quiet moments tap into the energy here.

There is Hidden Power.

There are ghosts too: reports of haunting at Avebury Manor by a phantom who wears a white hood and the old folk spoke of strange goings-on in cottages whose very walls contain stones from the original stone circle.

Something like fifteen miles away – as the crow reputedly flies – is another Wiltshire mystery: the Highwayman's Grave. The tradition is he was shot by the guard of the London to Bath stagecoach and buried face down with his head to the west. But Romanies believed an injustice was done. According to their gypsy bush telegraph he was no highwayman at all – and consequently they placed flowers on his grave.

Maiden Castle

More than once on an ancient landscape I have felt right at the edge of the unknown. On a visit to Maiden Castle I felt '. . . just one more thing to happen and then *breakthrough* . . .'

Maiden is an enigma: immense and open, yet retaining a secret something, an energising quality too. Above all, there is this powerful atmosphere, a feeling of expectancy – almost electricity – in the air. It is a surprise to find no records of hauntings of this lovely but curious landscape.

Four thousand years ago life was going on here, the location crowded with primitive houses and huts, a farming community requiring no defence except against wild beasts. Arthur Mee, researching his book on Dorset in the late 1930s, observed: 'This is Maiden Castle, the wonder of Early Britain, the finest prehistoric hill fort in this country, one of our earliest cities, forerunner of Roman Dorset.' Maybe it is this sense of the past, long and deep, which gives Maiden such a strong aura. Men and women were living and working here before the Great Wall of China was thought of.

I had an odd feeling on my first visit: the feeling that I had been there before – which was not the case. 'Maybe you had been here in a dream or a previous life,' suggested a psychic friend. Time in our ordinary everyday life unrolls like a piece of film but in places like Maiden Castle you half expect to find yourself in the past – and possibly some psychics may find themselves in the future.

AN OLD photograph of Maiden Castle showing the east entrance. It is a surprise to learn this location has no haunted reputation. Nevertheless Maiden retains an air of mystery and during the Hitler war some modern folklore evolved – that an underground passage, two miles in length, went from here to Dorchester and was used by the Home Guard.

Boscawen Ûn Stone Circle

There is a real thrill of discovery about some of our mysterious locations and Tamsin Thomas touched on the theme in her book *Mysteries in the Cornish Landscape*: 'It was so exciting to "discover" Boscawen-ûn stone circle, the almost secret circle which is reached by following a rough farm track outside the village of St Buryan. Exciting because these stones are not easily accessible, or visible from the road, like many others in Cornwall. On my first visit I had almost convinced myself that I had taken the wrong track as I wandered past trees warped and twisted by the harsh West Cornwall winds, when suddenly there they were, nineteen stones in the morning sun standing around a huge granite pillar which leaned dramatically towards the north-east. This phallic middle stone is said to represent masculinity, while another in the circle made from a large block of white quartz, portrays femininity. Both make this unique among the circles of Penwith.

'I found myself drawn to the middle stone – when I touched it it appeared to be giving off a comforting warmth, probably created by the morning sun shining on it. I know there are many sceptics who ridicule those who believe the stones have special powers or meanings, but does it not make sense for a woman to be attracted to that which represents masculinity?'

It was Charles Simpson who first told me about this magical circle, and there is a curious thrill as you walk inside and around these ancient stones. Monuments or temples? Places for astronomers or for the last rites? There have been various assumptions but these stones remain riddles in the landscape of Penwith. Dr Johnson probably got it right when he reflected: 'All that is really *known* of the ancient state of Britain is contained in a few pages . . .'

Despite our incomplete knowledge, I find visits to places like Boscawen-ûn really worthwhile – something deeper than mere interest and curiosity, more profound than an architect or historian discovering an old building.

For me anyway there is usually a refreshment of mind and spirit – the kind of experience religious people get from abbeys and monasteries. Provided there are not too many people about, the stones convey a message of some importance but we need to be quiet and humble.

THE MAGIC of the stone at Boscawen-Ûn.

THE BEAST
OF BODMIN MOOR

THE Beast of Bodmin Moor is an on-going story. He – or she – provokes different reactions. Some people believe the animal is a piece of fiction which will eventually grow into the folklore of the Moor. Others believe the animal is real.

In *Psychic Phenomena of the West*, published by Bossiney in 1994, I wrote of my encounter with a strange animal on the edge of Bodmin Moor – that was on May 19 1993. In this chapter I propose to concentrate on other developments in this animal mystery.

First, those of us who have seen this big cat-like character know he may have nothing to do with the supernatural. Secondly, there is almost certainly more than one of these animals and thirdly they have been around the moorland for several years. Moreover, very responsible people claim to have seen them. I have, for example, done book business with Henry and Rita Stickland since 1985. They run the Harbour Shop in Fore Street, Port Isaac and are two very down-to-earth people.

Here is Henry Stickland's recollection of their encounter: 'We were on an afternoon drive. Having been to Camelford our aim was to go to St Breward but we changed our minds and made for the Wessex War Memorial on the moor to give the dog a run.

'We turned a corner with a straight piece of road in front of us and an animal came over the bank on the Camelford side of the road. It looked at us and went up and over the opposite bank with no trouble.

'I slowed right down expecting sheep to follow what I thought was a black ram, but it had a long tail.

'My wife agreed about the tail also the ease with which it cleared the bank.

'I got out of the car and looked over the bank but could see nothing except sheep. They were making a lot of noise and seemed agitated. The date of this experience was the spring of 1989.'

An extra dimension to the whole story is that these animals have been seen on Exmoor and Dartmoor, probably proving a pack of such characters exists here in the Westcountry.

The following letter, published in the *Western Morning News* on August 3 1995, concerns a sighting in Devon:

'On July 10, my wife and I saw a "Beast" by the River Teign below Castle Drogo. We sat on a stile and watched it for a good ten minutes while it came to within 100 yards of us before disappearing over a bank into rough ground.

'It was exactly like the animal pictured (WMN, July 26).

'No one who has had a good view of one of these creatures could possibly confuse it with a domestic animal. I suspect they must be fairly numerous.' *H C Pratt, Lydford, Okehampton.*

A major development occurred in Cornwall in August 1995 when Barney Lanyon Jones, aged 14, and his older brothers Toby and Sam of Tremar Coombe, near Liskeard, found the skull of a big cat in the River Fowey near Golitha Falls below Jamaica Inn.

One man who had no doubts was Douglas Richardson, the assistant curator of mammals at London Zoo. After examining the seven inches long by four inches wide skull Mr Richardson said 'I believe this is the Beast of Bodmin Moor or one of them. There is more than one out there, that's for sure . . . It is definitely a big cat's skull. It is probably a leopard, possibly a puma. It still smells quite nasty which indicates to me that it died this year, possibly in the last two months.'

The Times of London, reporting the discovery on its front page, said 'The zoo's resurrection of the fabled Beast of Bodmin comes less than two weeks after the Ministry of Agriculture proclaimed the creature to be nothing more dangerous than a domestic pussycat. Rosemary Rhodes, one of many farmers on Bodmin Moor who claim that a big cat has been preying on their sheep and cattle, said "This is the confirmation we have been waiting for. We never had any faith in the Ministry of Agriculture's inquiry."'

Douglas Richardson said he thought the skull was most likely that of a melanistic leopard, popularly called a black panther. He was convinced by the two front fangs. 'The puma and the leopard are two of the most adaptable big cat species in the world. There is no weather our climate could throw at them which would faze them at all. They have no competitors and plenty of food in the form of deer and rabbits.'

In the same week of the boys' discovery, an entire family – four adults and four children – spotted a big black cat when walking near Siblyback Lake. The Unsworths, who formerly lived in Zambia and Kenya, said it was similar to some of the big cats they had seen when living in Central Africa.

But within a fortnight the big cat skull discovery was exposed as a hoax, specialists at the Natural History Museum identifying it as the skull from a young male leopard. Moreover the animal died abroad, possibly India. Entomologists discovered the remains of a tropical cockroach attached to dried membrane in the skull's cranial cavity. In their two-page report the Museum implied the skull resembled those 'often recovered from old leopard-skin rugs,' and concluded 'This particular leopard skull came to Cornwall only by human agency, and it is most unlikely that it had been in the river where it was recently discovered for any appreciable length of time.'

Douglas Richardson, for his part, conceded he had been misled into thinking the skull had come from an animal which had died recently by the softening effect of the water on tissue still clinging to it. Mr Richardson said 'The exposing of this hoax does not alter my opinion concerning the presence of big cats in southwest England. The evidence I have examined over the years, coupled with the first-hand evidence of some very credible witnesses, leaves me in no doubt about their existence. I am still very interested in assisting with a project that will put the matter to rest through the capture of one of these animals.'

Reports of sightings continued, with more in the month of August. On Thursday August 17 the *Cornish Guardian* published this front page story:

'A new twist to the Beast of Bodmin Moor mystery emerged this week with the sighting of a similar big cat at Tregrehan, near St Austell.

'Beryl Lambert and her friend Ingrid Legat-Crawley were on a Sunday afternoon blackberry-picking walk on a footpath close to the village when they spotted the creature walking alongside a hedge in a neighbouring field.

'Mrs Lambert said the cat was dark coloured with white markings on its back and was at least the size of a collie dog.

'She said: "It took us by surprise because it was definitely not an ordinary cat or dog.

'It slunk along the side of the hedge, then it looked around and saw us and disappeared into the field. We decided it was safer not to follow it into the field.

'Because of all the publicity surrounding the Beast of Bodmin Moor, I hesitated to report this sighting. But there is definitely a large cat-like creature roaming the countryside around Tregrehan.'

Then in September I had an exclusive interview with Brian Barker of Helland who is the son of a former gamekeeper, a man who has a good knowledge of animals and wildlife. Over a cup of tea he told me:

'I was driving down through Shell Woods, near Helland, early one morning in the spring of 1995, when I saw this strange animal sitting on a log where they had been cutting trees. He was black and miles too big for a cat. At first I thought it might be a black labrador but his head was too small and he had very pointed ears. I was high up in my lorry and had a very clear view; we were probably no more than ten paces apart. As soon as I touched my air brakes he was up and away. All the time I had been moving, he didn't seem to be worried. In fact he was looking straight at me and it was only when I stopped that he decided to move away . . . and in the blink of an eye he was gone. My view is that there must be more than one of these animals because two days later there was a sighting near Saltash and that's at least twenty miles as the crow flies.'

BOOKS ON THE
SUPERNATURAL

O NE of the greatest pleasures in the supernatural side of my life has been the building of a library on the supernatural – and the enjoyment and enlightenment from the reading of such books.

I am very fortunate in having two excellent sources here in the Westcountry. They are the Dartmoor Bookshop at Ashburton which sells secondhand books on a wide range of subjects and Midnight Books of Sidmouth, Devon who are specialists in secondhand books on the unexplained.

In any serious study of the paranormal and allied subjects, one is impressed by the calibre of the men and women who explore the edges of the unknown. Let us, for example, look at an outstanding man like Aldous Huxley who came from a pretty conventional background but became absorbed by the mind and the prospects of broadening the boundaries of human thought and imagination. He became fascinated by drugs and their effect on mental processes. He wrote several books on the subject and manipulation of the mind by drugs – providing the basis of his famous *Brave New World*. Further back in history we have Robert Louis Stevenson who recalled his dreams in such detail that he turned them into stories. It was, in fact, a dream which sowed the seeds for Robert Louis Stevenson's 1886 *Dr Jekyll and Mr Hyde*. Rudyard Kipling is another. Although not a special believer in psychic phenomena, in India

◀ *CHARLOTTE DYMOND'S lonely memorial on Bodmin Moor. A strange animal has been seen hereabouts.*

84

and the old British colonies he encountered scores of cases of extraordinary phenomena.

One of my first acquisitions was *The Haunting of Borley Rectory*, a critical enquiry made by three authors under the auspices of the Society for Psychical Research. Then in 1973 James Turner signed one of his very first copies of *Ghosts of the South West* for me. At the time he was living in St Teath village – but more of James later.

In my last supernatural title *Edge of the Unknown*, published by Bossiney early in 1995, I devoted a chapter to some favourite authors and books. That single chapter generated a number of letters, telephone calls and face-to-face enquiries. More than one person said 'When you write your next book, do include another chapter like that about other authors and other books.' So this section is a personal response.

As a ghost hunter for more than thirty years, I was especially pleased to get a copy of *A Dictionary of Ghosts* by Peter Haining, published by Robert Hale back in 1982. There have been many books produced on ghosts but the publishers claim this is 'the first work which provides a comprehensive and handy source of reference to the various types of ghosts throughout the world . . .'

Moreover it contains a rich harvest of illustrations. One of the most remarkable is the ghost of the Outback, a phantom which has been frequently seen in Australia, and photographed here by the Rev R S Blance in May 1956. Another is a quite extraordinary shot of ectoplasm being produced by Margery Crandon, the American medium. Furthermore the publishers underline their integrity by saying in the caption where a photograph is a fake. There is, for example, 'the ghost figure of the Virgin Mary which appeared in France in 1956 but which proved to be just a trick of light.'

Sonia and I are keen theatregoers; consequently we both enjoyed that very good book *Theatre Ghosts* by Roy Harley Lewis, published just across the Tamar by David & Charles at Newton Abbot in 1988. It is an interesting paranormal fact that many of our theatres are haunted – notably Drury Lane in London. *Theatre Ghosts* contains numerous first-hand accounts, a number substantiated by distinguished actors and actresses and theatre staff. Sir Harry Secombe, Donald Sinden, Evelyn Laye, and Margaret Rutherford are only some who appear inside these fascinating pages.

More than once, sitting in the theatre waiting for the curtain to go up, I have wondered why theatres, like inns, have such a haunted reputation. Could it be that so many actors were so happy on stage they are reluctant to leave it? I remember taking Alan Nance, the well-known healer and Spiritualist, to a haunted location and he said: 'This is such a lovely place I'm not surprised people who have died are reluctant to leave it for ever.' And maybe something of that lingers in and around our theatres.

I am writing these words at a desk which once belonged to the writer James Turner. James was a real literary all-rounder – novelist, poet, short storywriter, autobiographer and editor of a remarkable book in Frontiers of the Unknown, published by Souvenir in 1973. It is called *Stella C* and is an account of some original experiments in psychical research. Stella was a simple but well-educated young lady to whom odd things had often occurred. A chance meeting with Harry Price on a train journey to London led her to sitting for him thirteen times in 1923. In 1926 and 1928 Stella gave a further series of sittings attended by eminent scientists like Professor Julian Huxley, Professor E N da C Andrade and Dr R J Tillyard. James Turner edited the complete series of seances with additional notes, an appendix and a selection of Stella Cranshawe's correspondence to Harry Price. In the words of the publisher: 'The book, in a science hedged about with fraud and fraudulent mediums, is a memorial to truth and to the proper scientific approach to the subject of Psychical Research.' *Stella C* is certainly a book worth tracking down.

Another unusual volume is *The Company of White Knights* by Claire Mitchell published by The Book Guild of Lewes, Sussex in 1990. M C Mitchell first discovered she was psychic when she found her late brother-in-law writing a book through her hand. Many 'discarnates' have contacted Claire over the years and, as a result, she has a rich harvest of information from the fourth dimension. When Claire was only three years old her mother died whilst giving birth to a baby boy who also died. It was this brother, whom she never knew, who contacted her from the spirit world and the result is *The Company of White Knights*. There are insights into the lost continent of Atlantis, the origins of the Universe and the truth about Jesus.

As a Cornishman with Irish and Breton blood way back in the

family tree, I suppose it is inevitable that superstitions should attract like magnets. *The Dictionary of Superstitions* by Jean-Luc Caradeau and Cecile Donner is a mine of information. Published by Guild Publishing of London in 1985, it has been translated by Richard LeFanu and adapted for the British market by Jennifer Westwood. Omens are everywhere in life, and in this well planned, concisely written book the authors show us how we can become masters of our fate. The cynic will scoff of course, but for those interested in good luck and the breaking of bad spells this book is compelling reading.

Finally, a special favourite: *Haunted Britain* by Antony D Hippisley Coxe, a guide to supernatural sites. Published by Hutchinson & Co back in 1973, it's one of the best books of its kind and very well illustrated. Though I had some correspondence with the author, we never met – a pity because he lived not far away at Hartland in North Devon. In researching this book Mr & Mrs Coxe drove over 12,000 miles selecting and inspecting more than 1,000 locations, and it shows. This is a must for any book collector.

THERE is a strong British tradition that a robin coming indoors is a bad omen, foretelling a death. The old country folk had other theories about the robin. If they found him singing on the rooftop fine weather was on the way, but a robin singing in the hedge forecast bad conditions.

SUPERSTITION – OUR MENTAL APPROACH

THE supernatural, like hanging and hunting, sharply divides people into one of two camps: those for and those against. But perhaps the biggest divider of all is superstition. Many people believe superstition to be nothing more than 'old wive's tales' as they put it – and those probably are in the majority but there is a significant minority who think otherwise. These believe some signs are favourable, others malign. Whether we like it or not, omens are everywhere. They permeate our week from Sunday to Saturday.

I make no apology for devoting a chapter to this divisive subject because most people interested in the supernatural cherish a few superstitions – whether they admit it in public or not.

Moreover in this section I am generally concentrating on superstition in a very positive way, highlighting facets which traditionally bring us good luck, many of which have never appeared inside the pages of any previous Bossiney publication.

We begin our day by dressing. If we accidentally put on a piece of clothing inside out, this is regarded as very lucky; likewise odd socks and odd stockings. The old folk stuck to the letter in these respects, believing they were putting on the armour of good fortune for the day ahead.

Gamblers, by their very nature, are notoriously superstitious. Research into the gambling patterns of Monte Carlo showed there were special luck objects which gamblers carried with them: locks of hair, coins and four-leaved clovers. There was also an old tradition that having a pretty girl alongside you brought good luck; consequently many of the Edwardian gamblers paid chorus girls to sit with them at the gambling tables. Many, too, believed in 'beginner's luck' to the extent that seasoned gamblers bet along with a novice to benefit from his 'lucky innocence.' To be 'bombed' by bird droppings, particularly from a pigeon, is said to foretell good fortune – ever since the 1800s when a man at Monte Carlo had a handsome win after a pigeon had soiled his hat.

Luck and chance are closely related, but Douglas Hill in *Magic & Superstition* published by Paul Hamlyn in 1968: noted this important distinction:

'Luck is not the same as chance: it is chance that presents us with alternatives and luck that affects our choice. Luck, which we can sometimes control, or try to, guides us through the chances that present themselves during our lives. The unsuperstitious man tries to arrange his life-pattern so that chance plays as small a part in it as possible; the superstitious "trust to luck". Not for nothing has luck been anthropomorphised as a lady: just as we feel that she is with us, that we can understand and dominate her, she proves herself erratic, whimsical, capricious and wholly irrational. She might be there when we need her – if we are lucky.'

As a young man I remember hearing a magnificent Methodist sermon on the theme 'Life is not what we find but what we create.' Do we – to some degree – perhaps create some of our luck and some of our chances? I have a particular interest in sport and find the most successful sportsmen are usually confident and purposeful. Sportsmen, like gamblers, tend to be superstitious or, at least, ritual orientated. I have known cricketers and footballers who wanted to leave the dressing room last, and cricket captains who have stuck with a 'lucky coin' when tossing before the first innings.

Back in the 1950s when I became one of the first and youngest MCC youth coaches in the south west I was fortunate to meet John Guise, who had opened the batting for Middlesex and India, a knowledgeable man on the psychology of cricket and a first-class coach and writer on the technique of the game. He stressed the importance of 'relaxed concentration' and when I asked him the best thing a coach could do for a young player, he replied '. . . to encourage and instil confidence.'

Technically superstition comes in three elementary shapes. First, we have the omens; then the taboos (things we should not do, words we should not speak etc); and thirdly the rituals: the actions performed to bring about the objective or desired result.

Have I strayed from superstition? Maybe and maybe not, because mental approach and superstition are often connected, and on occasion amount to virtually the same thing.

It is an interesting fact that birds and animals have long featured in the realms of superstition and supernatural. White doves, for example, symbolize peace and friendship; whereas owls are regarded as birds of misfortune, often foretelling death or some disaster. Bats, those creatures of shadow and darkness, have a reputation for supernatural power; while the tiny robins are associated with fire and blood in legend and superstition.

Before the motor car and motorways, people said they had seen the ghosts of highwayman Dick Turpin and his mare Black Bess galloping on roads between London and York, and the old folk in Ireland in the earlier days told tales of the phouka or puca, a Celtic ghost which manifested itself in the shape of a horse and carried off the unwary on crazy rides!

For centuries the cat has been attributed with psychic powers, and it long has been considered that a cat who feels loved will bring good luck. Fate plays a big part in cats' lives – and our own for that matter or so I believe – and cats often appear and adopt us. There is an ancient tradition that many cats pick their homes and owners in this fated way; so much so many people decline to select a kitten from a litter – instead they stand near the kittens talking to them quietly. Sooner or later a kitten comes towards the stranger and *that* kitten has chosen its owner. In any study of magic the cat plays a significant role. In Britain the black cat is considered a very good omen and the animals were sacred to the Roman goddess Diana.

From cats to sneezes. I wonder how many people understand a sneeze followed by someone else saying 'Bless you!' is, in fact, all to do with magic. It has nothing to do with the hope the sneezer is not catching a cold. It all goes back to a primitive theory that a soul can leave the body through the mouth – that a sneeze may consequently expel it, leaving the soul vulnerable to the influences of evil. An extension of this thinking was the danger of the soul slipping out of the body during the hours of sleep. Therefore the primitives hated waking a sleeper suddenly and the reluctance to suddenly awaken a sleepwalker today stems from the same reasoning.

SUPERNATURAL EPILOGUE

There's always the problem of knowing how and when to finish . . .' Wallace Nicholls, the author, was sitting in a chair once owned by the poet Shelley.

Three and a half decades on I know perfectly what Wallace meant. Bringing this Bossiney's 233rd title to an end is difficult. As Sally Dodd finishes typing this manuscript, accounts continue to come in. This then is a kind of epilogue.

Here is an account from Sally herself: 'At Christmas my son Jason bought me cosmetics identical to those my daughter Lulu had bought me. Then he bought David, my husband, a jumper identical to the one Lulu had bought him. Jason also gave his father after-shave and toiletries identical to what I had given David. There had been no consultation whatsoever between Jason and Lulu and I had not discussed the matter of Christmas presents with either of them.'

Sally lives in Tavistock, one of the gateways to Dartmoor. Not far away is the village of Peter Tavy, the home of Joan Amos, a keen and knowledgeable researcher into UFO and other strange matters. Late in 1995 Joan told me: 'A strange case was reported recently of a half grown kitten missing from home found on a bleak wild and deserted beach three miles from its home. It was very distressed and the mystery is that it was found in a very inaccessible place . . . so isolated that the fishermen who rescued the animal couldn't figure out how it could have got there.'

Winifred Brown, a long time resident in North Cornwall, told me an unusual story. In the late 70s she and her husband bought a cottage not many miles from where I am writing these lines. 'I remember it very clearly,' she recalled. 'It was the first day in this cottage and I discovered a room at the end of the corridor . . . yes, a kind of secret room because I had not been aware of its existence on an earlier visit. Next morning I opened the door to this room and this small very low raftered room was filled with an old-fashioned bedstead and lying on it was the body of an old man with white hair . . . by the look of him you could tell he was dead. I rushed screaming down the stairs and told David, my husband, what I'd seen. We went back upstairs and found the room quite empty . . . no old-fashioned bedstead and no body. "You're getting overwrought" David said. Next day I went down to the village and met the vicar for the first time; I asked him about the family who had lived in the cottage. "They're all lying in my churchyard," he said, and he proceeded to describe the last person who had died in the cottage . . . an old man with white hair.'

I have just been reading a superb book on the paranormal. It's *The Hamlyn Book of Ghosts in Fact and Fiction* and was published by that company in 1978. Author Daniel Farson, who lives at Appledore in North Devon, on his opening page offered some interesting thoughts on that recurring question, 'What is a ghost?':

'We are moving toward an understanding of ghosts rapidly. I believe they will soon be as easy to explain as radio, television, tape-recordings or photographs – and will prove remarkably similar. The snapshot you take in summer to record your holiday needs a camera and a sensitive film. It also needs yourself and something to photograph. In a similar way, the ghost is an image that has left an imprint on a place that is exceptionally susceptible. Most likely it is a record of a moment of extreme emotional crisis which has taken place some time before. At the actual moment of someone's death this is so vivid it can be relayed like visual telepathy, then it fades.

'Just as the camera needs someone to work it, these ghostly images are only visible to certain receptive people at special moments in the right circumstances.'

The last decade has seen a rising tide of interest in all facets of the supernatural. I believe there are various reasons for this. First, many people feel unable – or unwilling – to use conventional paths leading to success or power or money – or all three – and instead they turn to the supernatural. But it is not all material ambition. There is a growing appetite in many individuals for psychic experience and a real desire for self-development.

CORNISHMAN Bob Fitzsimmons, left, beating 'Gentleman' Jim Corbett to win the world heavyweight championship. Bob, who was born at Helston, was a very superstitious man.

Looking for a manuscript chapter I came across a fragment of an old notebook, and found this recollection by Betty Paynter, later Betty Hill, who for many years lived in the Lamorna area of West Cornwall. Betty had a vivid childhood memory relating to that ancient stone circle near Lamorna known as the Merry Maidens. 'It was the first war,' she said, 'and the landlord ordered the field to be ploughed, and they started trying to uproot one of the stones when the lead horse suddenly dropped dead. The whole thing was called off, and everybody started crossing themselves.' The cynic of course, will dismiss it all as a coincidence, but I believe parts of the Westcountry landscape transmits a kind of supernatural message.

Maybe that is why so much has happened – and continues to happen here. I believe a major paranormal breakthrough will occur before long – and, on the evidence of the past, there must be a very good chance of it happening in the west.

January 1996

THE AUTHOR at his desk studying some autographed letters. Handwriting gives us insight into the character of the writer

ACKNOWLEDGEMENTS

THE heart and soul of these pages lie in the interviews – people who have given fascinating insights into their subjects. I thank them one and all. Thanks also for quotes from other writers – rather than rework their words I have let them speak for themselves and how well they speak. I am indebted to the editors of three Westcountry newspapers for kindly allowing me to use some extracts. The **Cornish Guardian,** *the* **Western Morning News** *and the* **Western Daily Press** *in their different styles personify the very best of Westcountry journalism.*

On the production side my appreciation goes to Sally Dodd for her usual immaculate typing and encouragement – and Angela Larcombe for her editing. Finally another big thank you to Felicity Young and Ray Bishop for giving such a strong visual quality to this title.

MORE BOSSINEY BOOKS ...

EDGE OF THE UNKNOWN
Michael Williams
'These investigations into psychic phenomena are some of the most fascinating in more than thirty years of ghost hunting.'

PSYCHIC PHENOMENA of the WEST
Michael Williams
The subject of a Daphne Skinnard interview in BBC Radio Cornwall.
'Michael Williams continues his well-known researches into the strange and the inexplicable ... cases range from Cornwall to Wiltshire ...' The Cornish Guardian

SUPERSTITION AND FOLKLORE
Michael Williams
A survey of Westcountry Superstitions: Interviews on the subject and some Cornish and Devon folklore.
'... the strictures that we all ignore at our peril. To help us keep out of trouble, Mr Williams has prepared a comprehensive list.' Frank Kempe, North Devon Journal-Herald

STRANGE STORIES FROM DEVON
Rosemary Anne Lauder and Michael Williams. 46 photographs.
Strange shapes and places – strange characters – the man they couldn't hang, and a Salcombe mystery, the Lynmouth disaster and a mysterious house are only some of the strange stories.
'... full of good stories, accompanied by many photographs of local happenings which have mystified.' Mary Richard, Tavistock Times

MYSTERIES OF THE SOUTH WEST
Tamsin Thomas of BBC Radio Cornwall
A tour of ancient sites in Cornwall and on Dartmoor.
'There is little doubt that Tamsin Thomas has become the 'Voice of Cornwall'. Ronnie Hoyle, North Cornwall Advertiser

THE CORNISH WORLD OF DAPHNE du MAURIER
Contains a previously unpublished chapter by Dame Daphne.

DISCOVERING BODMIN MOOR
E.V. Thompson

GHOSTS AND PHANTOMS OF THE WEST
Peter Underwood, President of the Ghost Club Society

KING ARTHUR IN THE WEST
Felicity Young and Michael Williams

We shall be pleased to send you our catalogue giving full details of our growing list of titles and forthcoming publications. If you have difficulty in obtaining our titles, write direct to Bossiney Books, Land's End, St Teath, Bodmin, Cornwall.